Tango Before Breakfast

Volume I

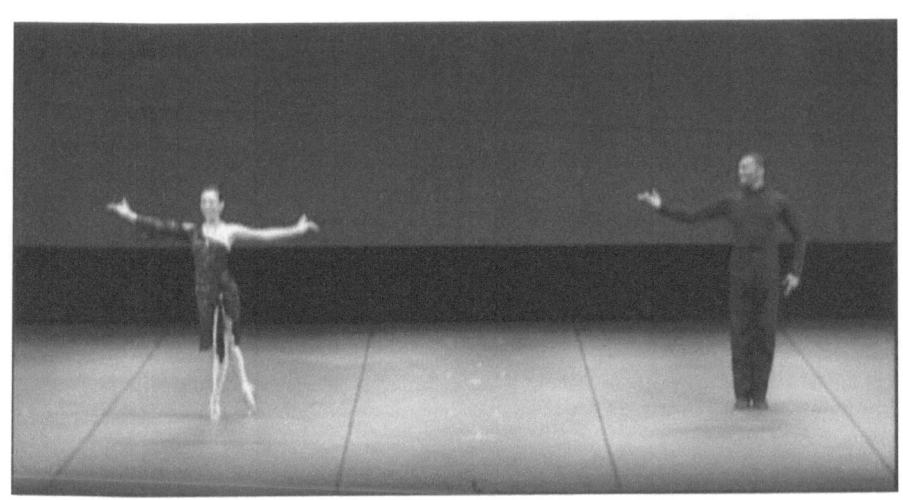

Tango Before Breakfast

Profile of a Choreographer

Michel F. Jacques

Library of Congress Control Number:		2010901450
ISBN:	Hardcover	978-1-4500-3467-8
	Softcover	978-1-4500-3466-1
	eBook	978-1-4500-3468-5

Rev. date: 09/19/2014

To order additional copies of this book, contact:
Xlibris LLC
1-888-795-4274
www.Xlibris.com
Orders@Xlibris.com
601233

CONTENTS

This book is dedicated to my father Emmanuel L. Jacques and in memory of my mother Macilia and my mentor James Banta. Also to my uncle Anthony Jacques, my brothers Robert, Denis, Felix and Gabriel . . . They always believed in me.

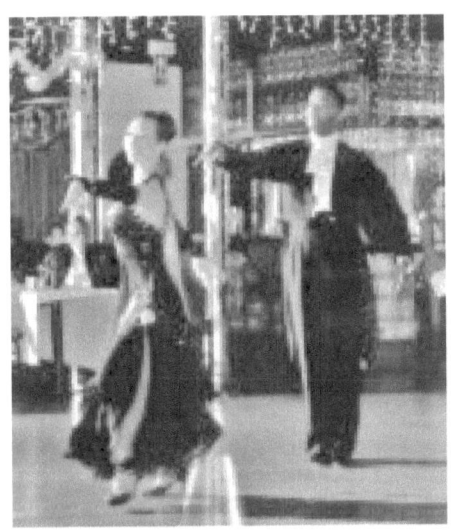

Preface

This first volume entitled Tango Before Breakfast is based on various essays written by numerous colleagues, dance practitioners and myself as part of my contribution to stimulate young adults to ballroom dancing.

My goal is to present the readers with a complete set of facts about myself in the industry of dance and film productions. And, the life style and involvement of my father in education and the political history of the country I came from. To show my admiration for other dance book writers and my appreciation to all my students and coaches who have been very supportive of my work for the past 25 years. To instruct the readers about the benefits, values of dancing and danger of learning to dance from non-certified instructors. My writing will generally interest all individuals with a passion for dancing.

My goal is also to help the American and international community friends who are helping in the rebuilding of Haiti have a broader view of the true cultural behaviors to expect. Who to trust and what to do with all the help they are giving to Haiti after the tragic earthquake. I am afraid the help we are receiving may get into the wrong hands. I hope they will embrace the National Dance Council Haiti Inc. and, understand that the dance community of Haiti is very poor, talented, and promising, very important to create the cultural identity of the country.

GOD GIVES, GOD TAKES. GOD's NAME BE EVER BLESSED. (JOB 1:21)

Profile

As a very young man, Francois began his career by learning basic dance movements at an early age in his hometown of Les Cayes, Haiti. To him, it was a very natural part of his lifestyle, and he considered it an entertaining and challenging hobby.

In 1980, he began his exploration of ballroom dancing at the Policard International Dance Institute in Port-au-Prince, Haiti. In a short time, Francois also developed his skills and talents as an on-air operator at Tele, Haiti, where he gained invaluable expertise in the field of music and video productions. To him, the role of dance is unique in maintaining a national and cultural identity. In 1984, Francois ventured to the United States to pursue and further develop his career in ballroom dancing.

He was invited to join the Arthur Murray Board of Educators by Mr. James Banta, in its rigorous teaching training program. With the demands and challenges of the program and as an associate social dance instructor, Francois achieved a greater understanding of the significance and impact dance would have on his life. He arduously studied and graduated with a music and video business degree (MVB) from the prestigious Art Institute of Fort Lauderdale, Florida, and developed a teaching style that conveyed to his students an understanding that musical rhythms are cultural representations applied to body language, emerging as communication of and for different ethnic communities.

His love for the art of dancing and the valuable knowledge acquired led Francois, in 1989, to conduct specific research studies in the international ballroom and Latin dance style, while he pored over volumes of written works on the origins of music and dance at Nova University's research library.

As a graduate in business ownership and management, his career brought him in contact with the owner of one of the largest ballroom/nightclubs in South Florida, Kay's Starlite Ballroom, Inc. in Hallandale Beach, Florida. Through his efforts at this establishment, Francois was instrumental in bringing the Haitian community together in celebration and demonstration of their ethnic and cultural unity. At this time, he began the development of a multicultural club organization that would embrace and bring together people of all ethnic backgrounds and offer the opportunity to exchange cultural diversity through the art of ballroom dancing.

Six years later, he successfully founded the New Millennium Youth Dance Sport Organization and registered it as a member of the International Dance Council. Its primary objective was to be the inclusion of dance as a fundamental part of education in the school system, beginning at the elementary level.

It is Francois's firm belief that, dance is the architecture of human movements. The analogy can be drawn to an architect who uses diverse materials to construct his creation in a particular place. Likewise, a choreographer uses intangible forms to create an impression in place and time. Their work is parallel and similar in the artistic sense. Professor Raftis Alkis, president of the International Dance Council said, "An architect has two dimensions: he is an engineer because he thinks rationally in contrast to the sculptor (who also creates his work in a particular place). Inasmuch, his work must have usable value. His creations are based on an understanding of the behavior of his materials".

As professor Raftis Alkis went on to say: "He is a technician and also an artist because he seeks to achieve an aesthetical, pleasing result. The choreographer, as an architect of movement, is first of all a technician. He knows the possibilities of the body (anatomy, physiology, and pathology). His knowledge is based on experience since he has sweated on the dance floor as a good architect has paced, for many years, on the scaffolding of his building sites. And of course, he must delight the spectators and make them think.

The making of both choreographer and architect require specific criteria: (a) extensive practical training, "taking the clay in their hands" or "dancing and teaching dance"; and (b) extensive study, research, reading, and reflection to gain the necessary theoretical equipment. How, then, can we explain the perplexing paradox: whereas there are university schools for architects in every country in the world, there are no equivalents for choreographers and dance teachers! One can count on one's fingers the countries where young people have the opportunity to simultaneously continue their dance studies, practical and theoretical, beyond the age of eighteen. "Further, even in the few available educational institutions that exist, they are underfunded and have scarce and limited resources."

Francois's primary personal objective is to be resolute and unwavering in pursuing the answer to the paradox. He is steadfast in his continued advancement of his knowledge in business management and media law, and he is eager to create advanced instructional dance and management programs for artists, dancers, and musicians in

Haiti, South Florida, and Europe. In Francois's own words, everyone has the ability to hear music and enjoy himself/herself without the need to visit a studio for a dance lesson, in the same way that everyone learns to speak and understand a native language prior to attending any school.

It is a natural progression of tradition and cultural mores. Dance, the first way to communicate, is the unique creation for peoples of all cultural backgrounds to express themselves through music. The multicultural study of dance presents a distinctive opportunity to enhance and enrich our understanding and communication with others. It is an exciting opportunity for our young people to combine their natural ability and talents with their knowledge of the fundamental subjects taught in school.

Learning this art form and exploring it to its highest possible level will offer our lives an added dimension with benefits beyond the physical and mental well-being. Learning to dance well is equivalent to speaking a language fluently. The skill of communicating in a language fluently could lead society to peace.

Over the past twenty years, Francois has been instrumental to the success of many ballrooms, clubs, and dance studios in South Florida by providing his specialized programs, management, choreography, music video production, and much more. In 1998, Francois introduced mambo/salsa and the Caribbean rhythms to the International Dance Teachers Congress in Hamburg, Germany.

He was the author of the ballroom compas/kompa dance, accepted by the International Dance Council at the world congress on dance research in Lanarca, Cyprus in 2005. He presented the mambo/salsa rhythm and the equivalent of music at the twentieth world congress on dance research in Athens, Greece. He believes that rhythm is a sacred and divine language within musicology and choreology in dance as its equivalent. For Francois, dancing at the wrong time to music can create disorientation of the brain setting, leading to lack of communication and discipline.

Currently, Francois is a registered member of the following prestigious organizations: National Dance Teacher of America (NDTA) Board of Directors, National Dance Council of America (NDCA), International Dance Council (CID), (IADMS) International association for Dance Science and medicine, (NDCH) National Dance Council Haiti (President/Founder).

This was an article in the Miami Herald about Club Kay's

The winter that Haiti crumbled, so did Fabie Bodek's illusion that she was anything but American. Returning home to Haiti three years ago as a translator for the U.S.-led multinational invasion force, Bodek, then 26, found no home at all. The country she

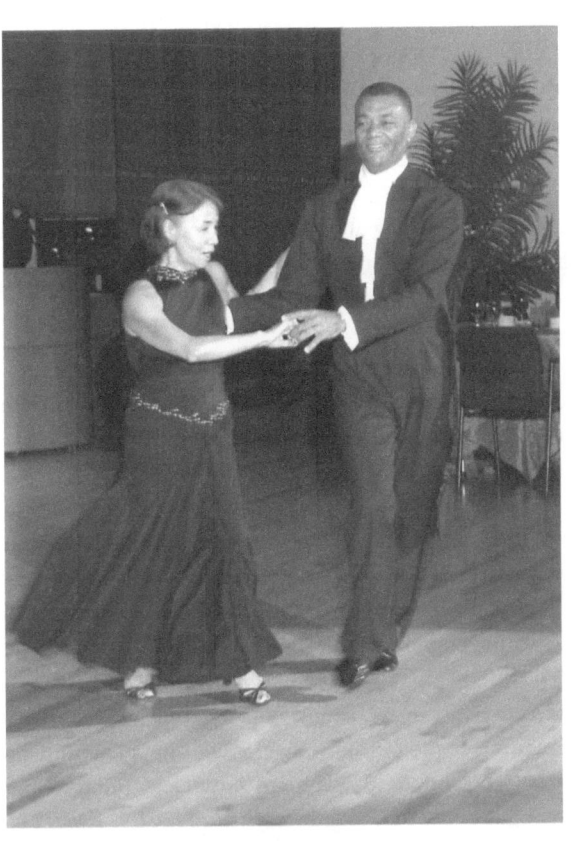

had imagined and idealized since coming to Miami when she was 10 was a country of strangers.

I felt as if life—the hardship of life—had hardened their hearts," she says. "I kept telling my friends who were with me, 'This is not what I thought it was like. They have changed.' And my friends said, 'No, they haven't changed. You just didn't know them.'"

Then one night, Bodek wandered into a shop in Port-au-Prince, attracted by the sound of dance music and the sign Policard Institut De Danses Internationales.

Unknowingly, she had entered a life-changing passage, one that would lead to a quirky ballroom 600 miles away in eastern Hallandale, where young black Haitians and elderly white Americans twirl side-by-side under twinkling lights.

Where white and black, young and old, American, Hispanic and Haitian learn not just the waltz, but a deeper understanding of an eternally mysterious process—the search for belonging.

A summer Sunday evening in a Hallandale Publix parking lot: Among the shoppers in shorts and T-shirts are couples in suits and cocktail dresses. From one set emanate scents of sweat and produce; from the other, scents of cologne and romance.

All night long, the handsomely dressed couples—an incongruous mix of mostly older whites with distinctly Northeastern accents, middle-aged Hispanics, and 20-to-30ish blacks chatting in Creole and French—converge several doors down from the grocery at a former movie theater, now called Club Kay's.

They are there because of a bridge constructed between their very separate lifestyles by Francois Jacques, a 38-year-old Haitian ballroom dance instructor. Through his nightly lessons and weekend concerts, Jacques practices a joyful philosophy: Dancing is a way of fitting in anywhere." Club Kay's 1710 E. Hallandale Bch. Blvd. has become a rare South Florida entity—a place where cultures don't collide, but blend.

The evening begins at 6pm with a deejay, Margo Newman, spinning salsa, rumba and other Latin/Ballroom tunes; two hours later, the mix relies on American/ European ballroom standards.

About two-thirds of the crowd of 300 or so is older white and younger Hispanic; much of the rest is mixed-age Haitian, and while there is little interracial dancing

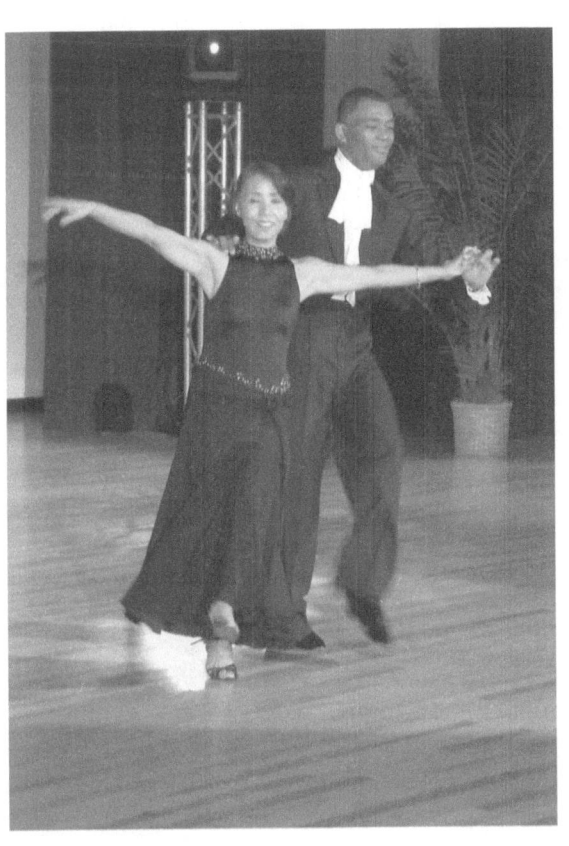

here, many already have twirled in each other's arms at Jacques Francois' $20-a-month, twice-weekly lessons.

The complete compendium of ballroom dancing happily unfolds—the gliding one-two-three beats of the waltz, the jaunty side-together side-together back-step of American swing, the infectious four-and-one TWO-three of the mambo; the stalking, deliberate slow-slow quick-quick slow rhythm of ballroom tango.

Professional-caliber dancers—there are many—stride smoothly, speedily along the dance floor's perimeter. Longtime couples comfortable with a few familiar steps and out-of-step novices are in the center or off in a corner.

Then, around 11, the deejay packs up her CDs and most of the older white couples go home. But the Haitians stay. And more keep coming, until they pack the place. The Tennessee Waltz and Stompin' at the Savoy give way to the soaring synthesizer and rhythmic, sensuous bass of taped Haitian dance tunes. At 1 a.m., legendary Haitian bandleader Coupe Cloue climbs onstage with his band of congas and guitars, and the joint literally jumps, shaking from the freight-train volume of the 73-year-old's famous compas.

The Haitians won't quit dancing until 4 a.m. At this hour, they have the place to themselves. The Americans are home in bed, too pooped to assimilate.

Ready to rhumba

About the same time Fabie Bodek's illusions about Haiti were collapsing, Frank and Joe Moretti's fantasies about the good life in South Florida were soaring.

The brothers from upstate New York had come to Hallandale to start a ballroom. Not a dance club, but a real ballroom, like New York's Stardust and Roseland—one with a bar, a menu and a big band. Neither Frank, 51, nor Joe, 59, is a dancer, but both grew up on Tommy Dorsey and love big-band music and the nightclub excitement that goes with it.

Everything seemed to fall in place. The Morettis found a defunct one-screen movie theater on East Hallandale Beach Boulevard that was cavernous enough to accommodate a 3,000-square-foot dance floor and stage, plus a 100-foot-long bar and a buffet. And it was just across the Intracoastal from Hallandale's oceanside condo canyon, where thousands of white, elderly, Northeast retirees were presumably ready to rhumba.

Then, like Bodek's illusion, the Morettis' fantasy began to fall apart. The city of Hallandale delivered the first bad news. The theater, so close to the ocean, lay upon

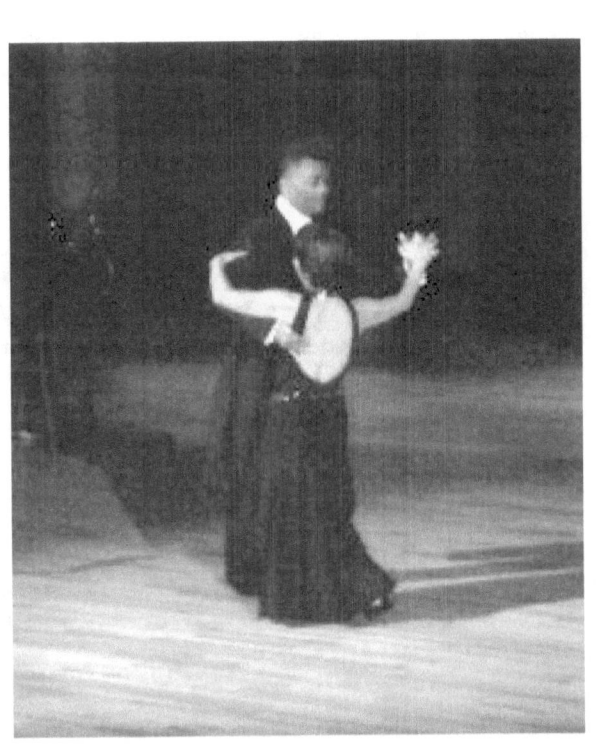

a base of sand. Inspectors feared the whole thing might collapse under the weight of cha-cha-ers. So they ordered the brothers to sink pilings below the theater, and a simple conversion suddenly bloomed into an $800,000 monster renovation.

The Morettis dug into their savings. During the construction of what would be the largest ballroom floor in South Florida, they also set about hiring musicians for a 17-piece band they would call the Starlites. Finally, two years ago, Club Kay's opened. And just as the Morettis hoped, hordes of dancers crossed the Intracoastal and crowded into the parking lot in all of their ballroom finery.

Then the brothers made another nearly disastrous discovery. Ballroom dancing actually is the most unromantic of romantic-looking pursuits. Though it seems effortless in Fred Astaire movies, it is a precise, complex art that requires a great deal of stamina and concentration—so much that beginner couples are warned never to look longingly into one another's eyes, lest they lose the rhythm or twirl into a collision.

Consequently, ballroom dancers have no more interest in eating or drinking between foxtrots than a sprinter would have between 100-yard dashes. And they don't much care for live music, either. Taped music has a more consistent tempo.

So the Morettis' Big Band, bar and buffet were nearly a bust. Until Francois Jacques danced into their lives, bringing with him South Florida's Haitians to the rescue.

Saturday Night Fever

In Bodek's words, Haitians are famous "party animals." They are not generally ballroom dancers, but they love live compas, the dominant dance music of Haiti, and will dance a simple Merengue all night long, between wining and dining.

The Morettis didn't know any of that, until Frank bumped into Jacques, who was working for an Arthur Murray studio and Luigi's dance club in Fort Lauderdale.

In Jacques, the Morettis found a trained sound engineer with the know-how to sign top-ranked Haitian bands and performers, such as Sweet Mickey and Skah Shah #1, Magnum Band, Tropicana etc, as well as a talented instructor who has trained many students to compete in dance competitions.

Jacques had come to Miami to visit his brother in 1984 and ended up staying. He had been working as an entertainment programmer for Haiti's main cable-TV company, TeleHaiti, broadcasting throughout Port-au-Prince American movies like all my children, Flash Dance and Saturday Night Fever.

Five years before Bodek had entered the Policard Institut De Danses Internationales in Port-au-Prince, Jacques had walked into the same place—the studio of Harry Policard, then Haiti's only ballroom instructor, and, he too, discovered his passion.

It wasn't the career in Media law that his prominent father—then the Mayor & prefect of Les Cayes on Haiti's southwestern tip—had envisioned for him, but it was a better bet than soccer, which Jacques also loved.

In Jacques' childhood, dancing had been a way of belonging. One of a family of 12 children, with an aunt living next door who had 13 more, he grew up in an environment in which friends and family got together often—either to play sports or dance.

"Dancing is a universal language," he says. "I can go anywhere in the world, the only black man on a ballroom dance floor, and through tango or cha-cha, communicate with everyone else there."

For the past year, he has been proving it.

Sometimes it takes some nudging. "Sur la piste! (on the floor!)" he commands, arranging the men and women in facing rows, then ordering the women to choose partners.

"At first, the Haitians and Americans tend to keep apart," he says. "But I make them change partners to learn the steps until pretty soon they're doing it without me telling them."

With men in chronic short supply, a few partnerless women often stand by themselves in erect dance position—left arm crooked as if around a shoulder, right arm extended as if reaching for a partner's hand, chin tilted slightly leftward—and practice with the rest.

Graceful dancers like Bodek, after seven months a star pupil, twirl arm-in-arm, hand-in-hand, with hapless Hallandale male retirees who look as if they forgot to take off their spiked golf shoes.

In at least one of the racially mixed matches, a couple ignored Jacques' strict prohibition against looking into each other's eyes—and the result was a waltz down the aisle.

Yvonne and Webert Benoit met over mambo/Salsa Class and recently married. "We met at the lessons, and discovered we had other things in common besides dancing," says Yvonne, who is American. Webert is Haitian. "We both do tae kwon do. How many people do you know who do martial arts and ballroom dancing together?"

Haitian gentry

When many of the Haitians explain the appeal of ballroom dancing, they say the music and finery remind them of the lifestyle they left behind in Haiti.

These are mostly Haitian gentry who held positions of influence and came to South Florida in the early '80s before the fall of the Duvalier regime.

Many have had to take lesser jobs here, but through hard work have assimilated into white, upper-middle-class neighborhoods from West Palm Beach to South Dade. They resent being asked if they are from Miami's working-class Little Haiti. "We're not off boats," Chantal Bonaparte says pointedly.

Bodek, whose family came to Miami in 1978, grew up in Miami Shores and attended schools in North Miami Beach. But somehow assimilation never happened.

"I was going to JFK Middle, which was a white school then, and I pretty much kept to myself. Now that I think about it, I was lonely, but at the time I didn't feel it because school was just for study and work, and at home I could have fun with my family. I had many nieces and nephews and we all lived together.

"I thought I did little outside my family because we weren't in Haiti. If I were there, I would have had friends and gone places. I always felt I was 100 percent Haitian, meaning that even though I grew up here, there was nothing American about me."

Then, three years ago, a shock: rejection as a Haitian in her homeland when she returned with the multinational force.

"People immediately spotted me as someone who had not grown up in Haiti," she says. "My ideology was not like theirs; it was tainted. For the first time, I felt like an American."

Bodek returned to Miami, where she now works as an ESOL teacher at Lindsey Hopkins Technical Education Center, with a revelation:

"I said to myself, 'This is my home. This is where I live and where I'm going to bring up my family. And I need to start acting American. I AM an American.'"

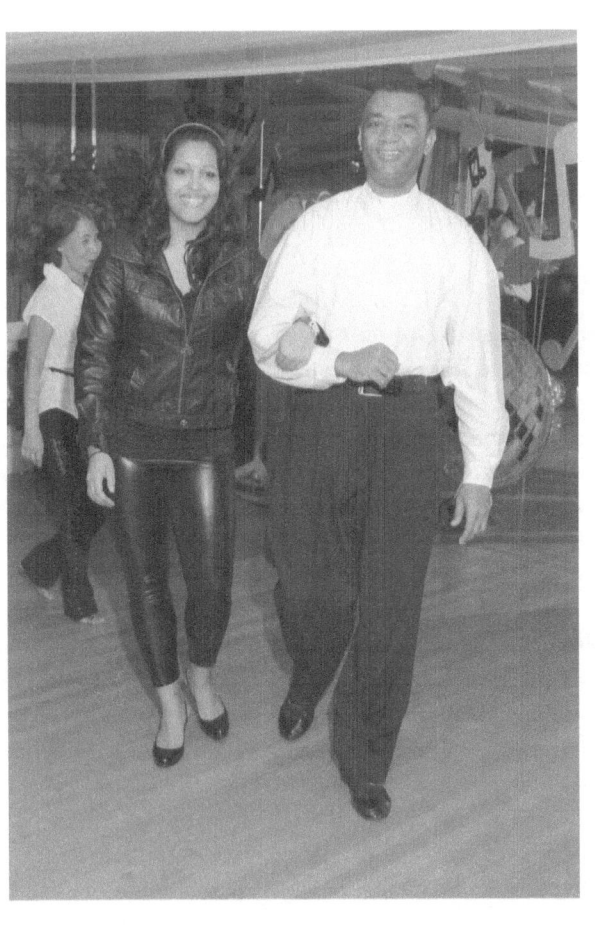

And remembering the magic of the waltzes and merengues she saw at Harry Policard's dance studio in Port-au-Prince, she sought out his protégé, Jacques, and became one of Club Kay's stars.

Recently, Jacques invited his students to a young nephew's Holy Communion party, partly, he says, so they could see a real Haitian Compas party, but also to introduce more friends and relatives to ballroom dancers.

"I like people and I don't like to be alone, and I want my ballroom family to be part of my real family in Florida," he says.

Meantime, Frank and Joe are diversifying. In addition to ballroom dance nights, Club Kay's has Latin Nights and Rave Nights. And Frank and Joe have just started another one, on alternating Wednesdays. Everyone's ready for "Iranian Disco?"

"Profile continued'

In all my teaching, I emphasize on the key elements in the construction of music that are necessary for every serious dancer to know in order to get all the health benefits dancing provides. These elements are rhythm, tempo, counts and beat value, mpm/bpm and high and low. Understanding how these elements affect a dancer's performance is critical to achieving success. The power of a dancer over his destiny depends on his ability to use his knowledge of music and apply it to his body, using postures and dynamic alignment to create some sort of etiquette to his movements. He is improving at the same time certain conditions in his life.

Many dance instructors teach listening to music the wrong way, using it for their own personal reasons. All rhythm comes from the cosmos and the divine. misinterpretation of music leads to lack of discipline and respect. People with that problem tend to develop ways to destroy the world settings. My job as a dance educator is to make everyone with an interest in learning aware of the danger and the value of this universal art as the visual form of musicology.

It is not easy to change bad habits; however, it is a unique opportunity for me to learn how to create a brighter future for my students and all dance practitioners. The levels of a professional choreographer are very complex and varied. At first, I was an interviewer, a salesperson with basic understanding of movement. Then I became an instructor with knowledge of ten steps in ten cultural dance art forms, following with the knowledge of ten steps in ten dances . . . an associate bronze instructor, a professional teacher of dance to a musicologist/choreologist. Dancer levels are also varied, depending on the individual's choice and needs. Some learn to dance for their own enjoyment, many people learn to please a date and enjoy themselves while others will learn to satisfy the judges as well as the audience and make a good living out of it all.

Dancing is a tool, a gift from God for people to overcome all challenges as well as physical and mental stress, a way to communicate. There is no rhythm without movements in dance; it is a sacred and divine language within us. Referring to musical instruments, the congas and drums are the two sacred instruments created for dancers to perform at a spiritual level. There are as many rhythms as there are cultures, as many postures as there are people; it is a cultural and national identity.

The unique identification sounds of the conga can only change in music by inspiring artist musicians. A great example is the compas/kompa social music/dance form of the Republic of Haiti made popular by the great musician artist Nemours Jean-Baptiste.

History of Ballroom Dancing

It is only when we study the ordinary pursuits of man that history becomes really interesting. One of the brightest threads in the fabric of man's evolution has been his love of dance. At all times and in all places, he has danced reflecting his joys, sorrows, passions, and longings. Dance is older than architecture, sculpture, music, or painting—older indeed than language itself. Dance has marked birth, marriages, and death. Celebrations for planting and harvesting also called for dance. Dance chased away evil spirits and cured the sick.

Ballroom dancing was probably the first form of dance that was invented purely for people's own amusement. In the fifteenth century, the basse dance brought important developments in dancing together; and first introduced in the courts of Italy, it spread through France and to England. It became very fashionable in the courts throughout Europe to dance, and those who aspired to court circles studied carefully the latest dances and copied them.

The year 1776 became the most important year in the history of ballroom dancing when the most spirited and ecstatic dance, the waltz, appeared in Vienna. This was the first real couple dance where dancers actually touch and had close contact. It was the twentieth century when ballroom dancing met the masses. Throughout the century, it has been the biggest pastime of every European nation. Surviving two world wars when it kept the nation's spirits alive, it became a way for a boy to meet a girl and for a working man to enjoy his leisure in the company of his lady

It became one of the few pastimes that a man could enjoy with his wife and has become a lasting symbol of wholesome family pleasure and enjoyment. Ballroom dancing is

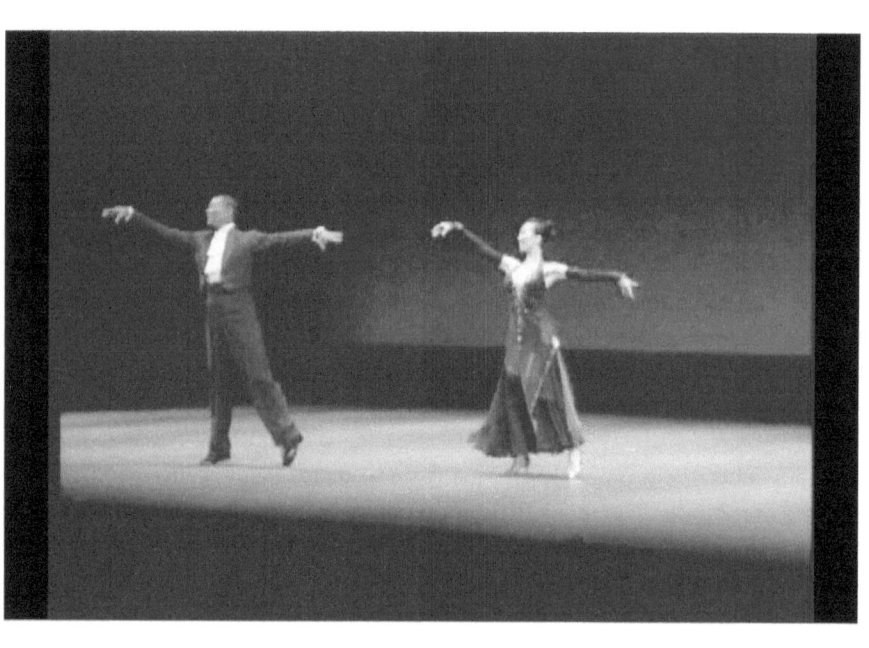

for all ages, all sizes, all classes, creeds, and colors; and I invite you to dip into the pleasure that is ballroom dancing. So start living. Start ballroom dancing. (Research made by David Robert and Nancy Kapsali)

Mambo/Salsa Rhythm
By: Michel F. Jacques

Salsa is a derivative of Mambo: We can give credit to the evolution of electronics in the music recording industries for creating new sounds for Salsa music. There are five elements that fall into the construction of all music. These five elements are essential for dancers and teachers to know in order to dance properly: (1) rhythm of the music—as a cultural identity, it is a specific sound within music that never changes; (2) tempo refers to the speed of the music; (3) count and beat value; (4) the MPM (measures per minute); and (5) up and down beats. Since all rhythms are related to the cosmos and the divine, dancing to the wrong timing of music is very dangerous. This one particular sound never speeds up or slows down. It always sounds the same from the beginning to the end of the music.

Before we start dancing, we need to be able to identify this specific sound in order to find the right beat value given to us by the high and the low beats. This is necessary to ensure that our movements will be in sync with the music. Not too many students are able to concentrate on music because they sometimes confuse rhythm with the term *tempo*. Mambo/salsa music is written on four main beats in a bar or measure. There is a space in between each beat that lasts just the time to say "and." The count is as follows: "and 1, and 2, and 3, and 4." The beats 4 and 1 give us time to change weight from one foot to another, creating a pause that characterizes the mambo/salsa dance. The tempo is quick and quick and slow, counted as 2 and 3 and 4 and 1. A breaking action occurs on the second beat of the music.

We can understand nightclub or street-style salsa where people dance to enjoy themselves with a continuity of body movements, going back and forth, creating a different style of mambo, which is not the same in ballroom dancing. In ballroom, all the movements are synchronized with the music using proper posture, alignment, footwork, and accurate amount of turns. Dancing is an art form to be learned and developed with time.

The role of dance in maintaining a national identity is unique in every country. In my early childhood, I faced a very big problem: I could not find the answer to what dancing was. I started learning how to dance over thirty-five years ago in my homeland of Les Cayes, Haiti, where dancing is part of life. Wherever the drum sounds, people tend to dance, which is not different from others around the world. Up to now, the meaning of dance was not clear to many people; however, I never met anyone who cannot learn how to dance or dislike it.

Some describe dancing as fun, as body movement, as a way to meet people, as exercise, as a therapeutic tool, as a way to express themselves; it's communication—the list of benefits one can get from it is endless. In a multilevel perspective, it is a language created for people of different ethnic backgrounds to express their joy, their sadness, their feelings, their fears, and inner needs—a universal visual art form within choreology, which is to dance to the equivalent of musicology.

"In traditional society, according to professor Raftis Alkis, dance is at the very heart of social life. In pre-industrial societies, monarchs, generals, and high priests danced; they danced not only at festivals, nuptials and places of entertainment, but also before battles, after the chase, inside the church, at public ceremonies as part of their education. It was as essential as speech. The first problem to be faced by students is the meaning of the word *dance*. Students must face the problem of searching for the meaning of the word dance. What we mean by dance today is not necessarily the same as what it meant in traditional society.

The word *dance* now tends to have choreographic connotations: referring to the execution of movements, doing the steps; learning the steps is synonymous with learning a particular dance. This is the case with many professional dancers who learn choreography, a series of more complex movements to be performed on stage and in many dance sports championships. It's viewed as purely psychokinetic phenomenon. Conversely, the meaning of dance is far more comprehensive; there should not be any distinction between dance, music, and song. Movement, sound, and words—all three are rhythmical. The words of a song, its tune, and the dance performed with it all comprise a single entity in men's minds. But serious consideration of this subject is nonexistent.

Since dancing activities are all around us, we treat it casually and pay very little attention. A multidisciplinary approach involving historians, ethnologists, sociologists, psychologists, and educationists to include ballroom dancing as part of education starting in elementary schools will not only help the dancers, musicians, and choreographers, but it will also make a decisive contribution to a deeper understanding of society in general".

When I started learning how to take my first step in dance, there were not too many of us who could dance properly to the music. Many of my friends dropped out of class because it was too hard to learn how to move in sync, even though we understood what the teacher was saying. I believe the level of distraction was very high. Imagine in the world today, less than 10 percent of the world population are learning ballroom dancing. About 90 percent have no clue about what is going on. Traditional/folk dancers feel guilty dancing out of sync to music. Ballroom dancers, tend to concentrate too much on their posture, how good they look, proper footwork, and dance characterization, so that sometime they go off the timing.

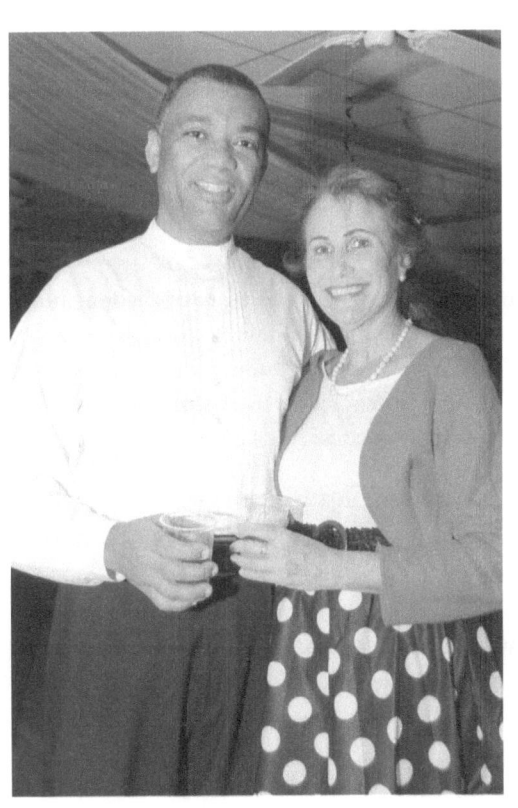

Learning to dance is like a relationship since, it has to do with the brain and all the joints of the body; you develop a skill to see the communication process between all the cells in the body and the flow or amount of energy needed for the moment; it has to be accurate. Intrapersonal communication deals with our own thoughts that can be transformed to words, giving us the written language. Whatever comes through our ears that we are able to translate into words sound more interpersonal. Music has a written form; we all need to learn how to read in order to make it understood to the musician who'll play it. If dancing is considered the interpretation of music, how do we know our movements are done properly, without understanding the basic foundation of music?

Children schooled in ballet and, or ballroom are more disciplined and are more respected than those in the street with no direction. Music has five elements within the construction; those key elements are essential for every dance teacher, dancer, and choreographer of all forms of dance in the world to master in order to dance with accuracy.

We should be concerned, though, with two types of rhythm: internal within ourselves and the one within music. The one within ourselves can be changed voluntarily; whereas the one within music is of course audible, fixed and specific, which is impossible to change. This is what makes us do things unsystematically, move around, express ourselves, and feel touches. It is important for all of this to be understood when it comes to dance.

Music is a natural identity that can become cultural and nationalized. It is a universal language, setting the characteristic of a certain inspirational behavior of a unique dance art form. Dancing is created with movements of our body, expressing various gestures while drawing graphic designs of the footwork on the floor to fit a number of bars in the music from the beginning to the end. This is what set the characteristic of this cultural art form in dance.

Natural behaviors of the people who study dance can only be changed by changes made in rhythm or speed of the music being played. Let us take the opportunity to introduce the compass (kompa), known as a mathematical piece of instrument in architecture. We use it to create variety in blueprints for building constructions. Nemours Jean-Baptiste and many Haitian musicologists of the past made specific changes in the way music was played in the island of "Saint-Domingue".

Before and after Haiti's independence, music was just an interpretation of various musical forms: Indian, Spanish, French, European, and African origins. The idea of the independence created the need for a true cultural identity for the people. It was not possible for Haitians to earn or simply claim an identity. The question had

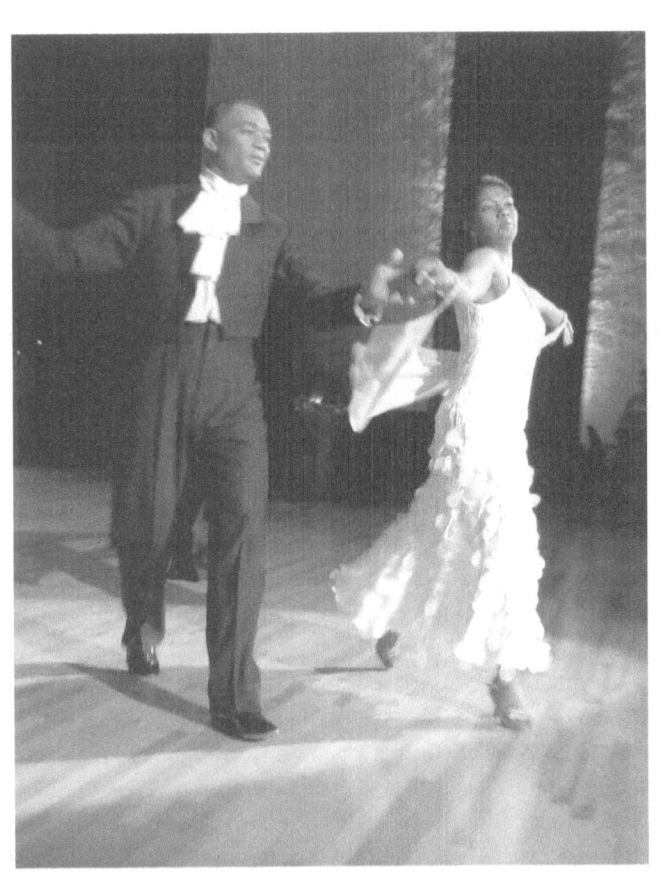

always been "Who are Haitians?" These musicologists of the past created a musical art form using various types of rhythm as the instrument that would represent and identify the people.

Kompa is the appropriate name given to the Haitian national music and social dance art form. It's a mixture of Afro/Latin with some sort of European flavor. The rhythm is mixed with mambo/salsa, cha-cha, samba, disco/hustle and Afro—more sensual than the Dominican-style merengue. Nemours wanted to stay apart from the merengue style of the past. Nemours was very upset, sick inside because of the infringement of so much Haitian music; Untouchable sounds immigrated elsewhere. They cannot claim them as part of their heritage. A *meringue* is "a dessert topping consisting of a baked mixture of stiffly beaten egg whites and sugar or a shell made of meringue and filled with fruit or ice cream. *Merengue/Compas* is a ballroom dance of Haitian and Dominican origin in 2/4 and 4/4 time. Different than the traditional way, in which one foot was used to be dragged on every step".

Some years after its discovery by Christopher Columbus, the Island of Hispaniola was the place for hardworking Africans to come for work and learn social networking. They came from various tribes in Africa with no written form of communication. They were forced to study the French language, a better bet for a new civilization at that time. It marked the beginning of a new society (the creation of a new type of social democracy) for those who had the opportunity to learn how to read and write French. Music and dance were the major fluent form of communication they used to express their feelings of joy, anger and resentment. The Afro rhythm traveled to the Island of Cuba next door and soon became a mixture of Afro-Cuban, developed all over the world. It is one the richest industries of Latin America today.

The power of the Spanish written language and the knowledge of the people made a quick transition to the educational system of all Spanish-speaking countries and the world to follow. The sound of all the Cuban music became the Basso-Nova, Rumba, Mambo, Cha-Cha-Cha etc. Today, new generation of dances are Salsa, Zouk and Bachata. You can always find the origin of the music by the way people dance to it. The body expression cannot hide the truth in terms of identities. What people ignore the most is their posture, which describes our genetic and cultural heritage.

What makes life interesting to me is how the new generation of dancers practice the art of dance by the way they feel about what they see, hear and study. Some do not believe in tradition, they prefer to believe in a twisted history of music and dance. The birth of the compas music/dance art form will prove to be a great inspiration for all artists, musicians and dancers. There is a great possibility for the next generation of Haitians to gain recognition as one of the purest and hardest-working on earth. However, we need to win the war on an artistic level first by making popular all our valuable art forms, adding to the education of the youth. They will learn and create an opportunity for the Creole language and the kompa Music/dance to be accepted as a cultural exchange.

The more you write, read, and speak the language of dance, the more useful you are to society, the greater of a community, city, or country you are able to represent. Musicologists all over the country of Haiti took pride in playing, promoting, and offering the kompa music to the rest of the world as the Haitian socio-cultural dance music art form. This highly complicated mixture of the merengue, cha-cha, samba, salsa, swing, and hustle tempo gives credit to all that is Afro-rhythm. We as Haitians need to sit back to see for ourselves that music and dance is considered one of the richest products of the nation.

Socrates learned to dance when he was seventy years old; he thought there was something missing in his skills of communication. My partner Fong, is very happy to help in the promotion of this new concept of dancing to the kompa music. The next generation of social dancers and choreographers all over the world with the same common goal will learn it and pass it on. They will be able to continue working in unity to develop a worldwide recognition of this new customized behavior.

Our history today simply, makes us believe that Toussaint Louverture and Jean-Jacques Dessalines are among the great heroes who led Haiti to independence in 1803. George III, the king of England contributed a lot to make this dream come true for all of us, by blocking all the ports of entry into the Island of Saint-Domingue. This stopped the colonial army of France from getting in to defeat the indigenous army—who also deserved some credit for what we are today. Circumstances often change a situation. Individual interests are the vehicle of all human actions. This fact is the same for one person as it is for groups and countries.

Saint-Domingue was the richest of all the French colonies. An independence movement started by Toussaint Louverture caused his arrest and deportation to France where he came from. The indigenous army would have the same opportunity; they should be treated the same as the colonial army of France. Jean-Jacques Dessalines took over Toussaint's idea that paved the road to independence in 1803. In January 1804, Saint-Domingue became Haiti, free from the French governance. There was no spontaneous victory. The English army was defeated in reality by United States with the help of France. They blocked all the port of entries to Saint-Domingue. That was exactly what caused the defeat of the colonial army from winning over the indigenous army of Toussaint Louverture and Jean-Jacques Dessalines.
END Here!

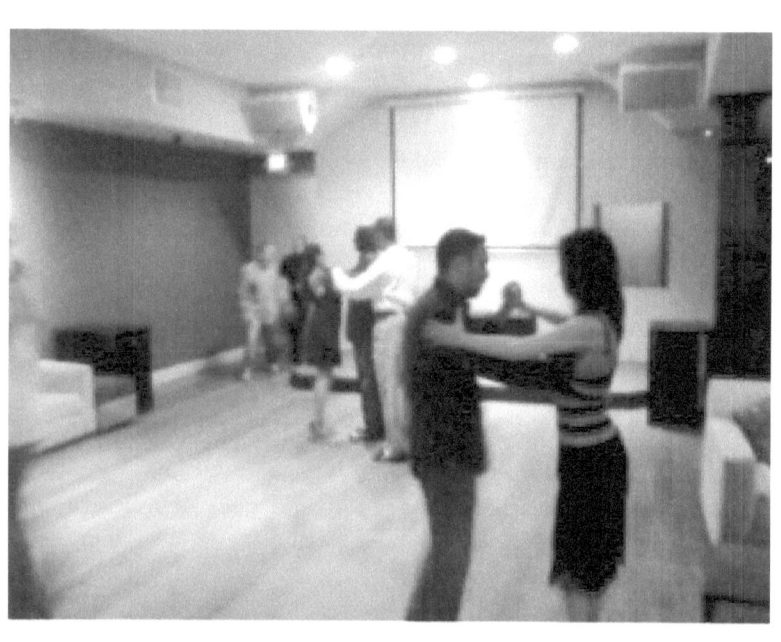

The English colony, through George III the king of England, took the opportunity of revenge to support the idea of Dessalines leading us to be independent. I myself, have to admit after God and Destiny that if it was not for England, the indigenous army of Dessalines would not have been victorious. This is where I have to stop writing about the independence of Haiti.

According to an international law, when a third world country cannot organize itself, the closest more powerful nation has the right to step in and take control, that is the reason the United States occupied Haiti in 1915. Naturally, as all other nations would do, the United States tried to reform the country. They reorganized education, created the agricultural school (Damien), and urban and rural public schools. They rebuilt the roads for easier transportation, reformed the army force, turning them out to be very educated and well-trained. The roads that were not paved were in good shape and the financial system was organized as well.

In 1934, a nationalist government, through the leadership of Estenio Vincent, was established. He obtained the dis-occupation of the United States government. Then, what happened? . . . from Estenio Vincent to Magloire Paul Eugene laid the foundation for what we now know as Haiti. Many people today still cannot agree among themselves about how much the United States did for Haiti. The question is who had helped the generation before us to reorganize the people? I believe it was the Americans. Naturally, their army was acting with force, which is exactly what everyone else would do.

However, if the people before us had the knowledge to maintain properly what had been left by the USA after the occupation, Haiti would never be in this situation—to depend on others for everything we need. We all need to think to come up with a national vision, unite ourselves and work to make it happen. Because of the existence of UNO, our close friends have no choice but to give us assistance and protection. However, it is up to us to manage the help we are getting from overseas.

With the power of education and the knowledge acquired, we will certainly be able to produce and duplicate all the help we are getting from outsiders. Now, many of us blame Dr. Francois Duvalier. Who had given the power to him? Written history simply said that Francois Duvalier was a medical doctor who studied at Michigan State University School of Medicine. He was hired by an American organization to work in Haiti. He had discovered a medication to cure some sort of sickness that was killing the Haitian people at that time. A vaccine he used to restore the health to Haitian people who were sick. He traveled to over 550 different towns all over the country especially the rural areas. He was working in conjunction with the International Institute of American Affairs. They all worked together and completely eliminated the whole problem in about one year. Everybody was healed because of this medication, a great relief for the government at that time.

It is not surprising for the generation under the ages of fifty-five not to know what had happened. They ignored the good stuff to promote all that is bad. Does everyone over fifty-five forget all the good developments that had existed in the past? I doubt it. My dad was a school professor; he had chosen to work alongside Dr. Francois Duvalier during his trips all over the rural territories. He was placed in the southern department of the island; all the people he questioned answered, "It was the Haitian army who gave power to Dr. Francois Duvalier to become president for life."

The peasants from the south voted Dr. Francois Duvalier because he had given them their life and health to be on their feet. The other candidate gave them food. So they voted fifty-fifty for both candidates. According to my father, it was the first time in Haitian history that a president had been elected with so many votes by the people, who had to fight together to live. Dr. Francois Duvalier spent fourteen years in power with a minimum of military assault, as president for life. He left his son in power who was an adolescent in politics at that time yet, stayed in as president for life reigning for fifteen years. The whole army stood behind him; everything was cool in those old days. However the simple idea of president for life was killing him, so he decided to leave the country and settle in France in 1986.

The Spanish people who occupied us before were in love with the Indians who were not used to the hard labor of agricultural and gold mining (Saint-Domingue was full of gold mines). They were dying by the millions. They did not have any other alternative than to bring in workers from Africa. They went there in search of tough agricultural workers to take over the working force, replacing the Indians. Unfortunately, black people at that time were not considered equal. They came to the island from over seventeen different tribes. They did not have a written form of communication between themselves. Therefore, they could not work together.

Being in the same boat, they ended up with the obligation to socialize together, creating a language that combined French, English, Spanish, and Portuguese with their own words which became Creole. It was absolutely impossible to write. However, living in Haiti with a language that had no written form of expression, it was impossible to be part of the schooling system. They had no choice but to learn French as the official language.

Today, we need to give thanks to the American doctors of education who produced the Creole visual graphic to be part of our educational system, which makes it possible for today's generation to be able to learn in school. People all over the world now have the opportunity to know Haiti and study Creole. The system contains words in different languages that sound similar: *wa* = *roi* (Creole/French), we = *oui* English/ French. I feel the graphic should be designed or studied with more French words that sound the same in Creole. *Pantalon* is a French word similar in Creole as well as *chaise*, etc.

There are many French words that should be integrated in the official Creole language. It would create a better opportunity for the youth to be fluent, making it easier and faster to learn both languages. It was a great decision for the governments to accept this project, which makes it possible for the next generation to express themselves fluently, be more organized and more productive.

The African tribes have never been in agreement with each other. The slogan UNION FAIT LA FORCE (UNION MAKES POWER) was said just to show them the necessity of working and being together, to look at themselves as one tribe. Saint-Domingue is where they have to join hands to obtain freedom of equality.

Effectively that was exactly what led the country to gain independence in 1803 at Vertiere, and after all, what happened? Despite it all, as great musicologists are saying, the "union fait la force" has never been an option for the Haitian people. They brought in a story between blacks versus whites, blacks versus mulattoes, and all kinds of repercussions, which continue to be a problem and is surfacing even today.

There are so many talented Haitian artists out there without hope of getting the recognition they deserve, they have never been given a chance to claim ownership of their own creations. Many have no choice than to hide their Haitian identity to be accepted and gain glory. Celia Lacroix died, unable to claim her true heritage. I am proud as an artist choreographer to have had the opportunity to pursue my schooling in the United States, to be able to know the exact me, to be able to work with the most talented musicians/dancers of my own country who helped me realize how diverse and rich we are in culture. I had never experienced what our history was all about until 1984, the year I landed in the United States aboard Eastern Airlines.

I was always too busy pursuing my education. I had the privilege to study with some of the greatest ballroom dance educators of America and to have a lifestyle similar to what I left behind in Port-au-Prince, Haiti. When I was very young, I realized that English should be my official language. Because of this, it was easier for me to continue my high school I.C.S

I studied English as a second language at Jamaica School of Business. I was fluent enough to teach English to beginners and assist in the management of the sister school in Ruelle Jeremie (1980-1984), while developing interest in film production, working for a cable television station (Tele-Haiti). My main reason for coming to the United

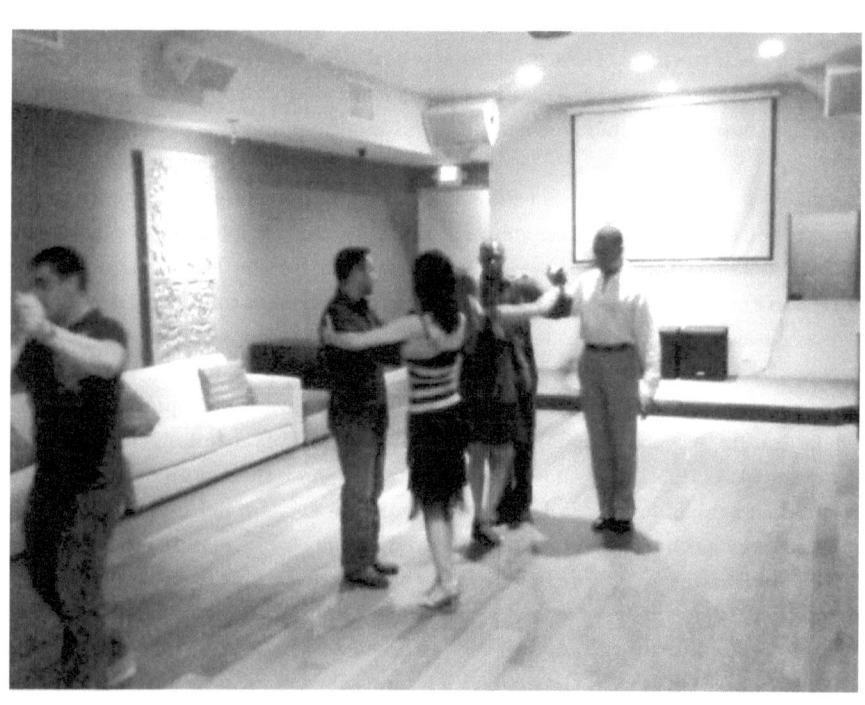

States was to become a film director. On my way to Los Angeles, I was pressured by my brother Gabriel to come to Miami, Florida to be with him. I visited one of the Arthur Murray Dance Studios and, I eventually decided to stay in Florida and become part of the "Ballroom Dance Family". It ended up costing me twenty-five years that I could have used pursuing my first dream of becoming a filmmaker.

God and destiny led me to obtain my first associate degree in ballroom dance education and an associate of science degree in music and video business (MVB) at the Art Institute of Fort Lauderdale, Florida. All these together led me to manage and develop the first multicultural club organization of South Florida (Kay's Starlite Ballroom). The Haitian diaspora joined hands and took the opportunity to promote our cultural diversities, more precisely the kompa music/dancing in Hallandale Beach, the upper class of little Haiti on weekends only.

I would like to mention that my mother never praised us for having good grades in school; it was something automatic when growing up, learning in our own father's school. Instead, her exact words were "I will be proud of you when you enter the university school of life." I can remember when my brother Gabriel opened his first auto driving school, she was laughing and congratulated him for entering university of life. I believe it is something we all, in the Jacques family had to prove to our parents. Gabriel was the first in the family to become his own boss, which even now, creates joy among us.

My dad never said much, but when he did, he gave us good advice. He always said that intellectual properties are more powerful and valuable than gold in the bank. I thought opening a multicultural club organization, the New Millennium Ballroom which would bring people from all over the world to Hallandale was going to make me a millionaire. But, I was too involved in helping in the development of the Haitian community needs, the promotion of our own identity through *Kompa* music. I have no regrets I consider also, my contribution to other community services promoting diversities, worth more than having millions in the bank. The entertainment industry of Haiti is booming. The kompa Music Festival is the largest Haitian cultural event in the USA, the proceeds are helping many people in South Florida and Haiti now. The city of Hallandale suddenly became a very important city in South Florida.

People from all over the world came to Club Kay's and later to the New Millennium Ballroom to celebrate their own cultural heritage. I was able to do my research in the origin of music and dance to learn about different cultural backgrounds, being able to work with people of diverse paths and class. Club Kay's was a different type of club—a unique classification of nightclub in the state of Florida. This type of club originated in Haiti and is now used by many ballroom club owners in south Florida.

This helped me remember the kind of Haiti I left behind, still forgotten to many people around the world, a country worth visiting one day. The beauty of this Island is the sunshine, the beaches, the donkeys, the big rivers, the mountains and waterfalls. The most valuable asset now, I presume, to combat poverty is proper management of all our cultural art forms and artist musicians, painters and dancers. It is possible that 90 percent of the youth in Haiti are living in hunger—they need help. They are also in search of direction and instructions to attain a new identity.

Now is the time; I feel I am about to enter the university of life. Many of the most talented hopeless people of the country are living their life by playing music and dance. Most of them read, write and speak creole fluently. I believe there is hope, the hope to launch a national dance council Haiti (N.D.C.H) that will provide them with a proper music and dance training management program in the school system. This will produce better interactive products for television to be sold to millions of people who are willing to help or invest in NDCH projects. This is for all who are concerned in helping bring about change in Haiti.

The friends around the world who will donate $20 a year to this organization will receive in return one DVD showing the progress made. That's enough to raise funds to help specific government projects to attract more tourists to the island. We can do it and together create a new identity for the people of Haiti.

Dance Industry in Haiti

Currently, 368 ballroom dance schools are now in operation in Haiti.
A minimum of one thousand ballroom dance teachers are earning an income.

Membership goal of the National Dance Council Haiti within five years should be one thousand members. We will be able to provide dance training to one thousand elementary schools (with government approval), starting in elementary school, encompassing four grade levels, two hours of instruction per week with an average of thirty students equal a potential of 120 students per school, learning ballroom dancing.

First National Dance Competition for Haiti Junior Division

Approximately 120 students by 1,000 schools equal a potential of 120,000 youth competitors. It should generate 6,000 couples competing in junior division only.

Amateur Adult Division

Projection: 368 schools will develop 3 competition couples per ballroom school equal 1,104 adult couples.

Professional Division

If each studio would send one couple that would equal 368 professional couples.

Pro/Am Division

Each teacher should have 3 students competing, multiplied 1,000 by 3 students equal 3,000 Pro/Am couples.

The total Haitian competitive couples in all divisions should be approximately 10,472 competitive couples.

National Dance Council Haiti is in search of investors, shareholders and members to form a management committee. We will have enough money to pay these teachers to teach in the public/private institutions to make this a reality for our beautiful country. Let's join hands to help our government.

Sacred Hidden Thoughts

The Art Museum of Fort Lauderdale, Florida, is very diverse in collection. The museum combines major works by established national and international artists with paintings, photographs, and sculptures by artists based here in South Florida, which were in exhibit. From the collections, the three that fascinated me the most were Cornelia Parker, Ross Bleckner, and Edouard Duval Carrie.

Cornelia Parker

In the *Thirty Pieces of Silver* in which Cornelia Parker is telling us about the possibility and value of antiquity, pieces of material that would have been lost and worthless that have a golden value, "Piccirilli, N." Cornelia Parker's work is about the resurrection of valuable creations, giving us a new direction. Her works are all about the potential of material; she brings to life things that have been killed. I can imagine that she's telling us how much value we put to material properties than to ourselves as humans. Cornelia is referring to the story when Judas betrayed Jesus for thirty pieces of coins, another way for her to test the boundaries of the physical realities of materialistic value over human, "Current Exhibit".

Ross Bleckner

Ross Bleckner is my second fascinating artist from the collections *Before and After Being Young*, 1987, oil on canvas. Bleckner is explaining what happens before and after a broken heart. A sudden change of mood, the subjects are more symbolic than direct. His works are intentionally and visually elusive; you constantly change focus ("Current Exhibit"). His collection gave me a feeling as if I had had a glass of wine; I was lost for a minute, and my sense of focus was on and off. As he said, his art is about how the shapes form and unform, how they dissolve and reassemble.

Edouard Duval Carrie

The most fascinating and incredible Haitian artist is Edouard Duval Carrie, whom I happen to know personally. In his exhibit, according to Steinbaum, he bespeaks an ineradicable connection to the island of Haiti where he incorporated the voodoo as a Haitian form of religion in his visual drama. *The Migration of People from Haiti to Miami Is a Long Story.* People are constantly searching for this untold story, why Haitians are constantly leaving the country by boat to Miami. Haiti is probably the main free port of entry for African workers to the USA, a type of trade money-making business from the slave's area still exists today.

Being born and growing up there, in my observation, I look at voodoo as a make-believe philosophy, a misunderstanding of spirituality in religion, a custom of living and practice by the less educated people. Knowing that, the independency of Haiti remains to be the people's pride. For the believers, the instantaneous victory of the independency was a sacred and divine movement.

When the indigenous army, less powerful at that time, won the independence of Haiti against the colonial army of France, who was more powerful, they believe it was voodoo tricks. Therefore, the people worshiped the spirit of the great General Toussaint Louverture, who was black and of French origin. The independence of Haiti was just an idea followed by Jean-Jacques Dessalines with the help of the English army, which created a long everlasting history for Haiti.

I have to say if it was not for George III, the king of England who blocked all the ports of entry to the Island of Saint-Domingue (Haiti), holding back the colonial army Haiti would never be independent today.

The written Creole language was nonexistent. The educational system had never been reorganized, leaving the older generations with different beliefs than the rest of the organized world. Toussaint Louverture started the independence movement for black Haitians to have the same treatment as the white and the mulattoes. How can one imagine Haiti, the richest of the French colonies, as the poorest and still unorganized? It is possible that the French wrote a make-believe history and created a pride for the people to study and practice. The African workers to Haiti didn't have a common written language; they have to spend two hundred years after the independence trying to understand each other.

Today, less than 60% of the people can speak and write French fluently. Lack of communication still remains prevalent. The United States was the first country who helped in the organization of the system during its occupancy in 1915, making the Creole a written language, which marked the greatest hope toward a new civilization for the coming generations. Many had to escape the island from all those happenings to Miami in search of work and better education . . . a new life. Edouard Duval Carrie, a well-educated artist of Haiti, understood all this and strived to explain through his works the effect of seaborne commerce and the cosmopolitan ideas ("Stumpt E"). "Its wealth made possible the leisure without which the life of true art and philosophy could hardly develop in the island of his birth, and the broad-mindedness and inquisitiveness of the people created a congenial atmosphere for the intellectual activity that is to become voodoo".

Bibliography

"Current Exhibit." The Museum of Art Fort Lauderdale. Wed., 25 Sept 2009.

Piccirilli, N. "Friday is Texture Day." The Museum of Art Fort Lauderdale, Florida. Lecture presented on September 11, 2009. www.moafl.org

Steinbaum, Bernice. The Museum of Art Fort Lauderdale, Florida. Viewed on Sept 11, 2009.

Stumpt, E. *Philosophy: History and Problems.* 3rd ed. New York: Pearson, 1987. Print.

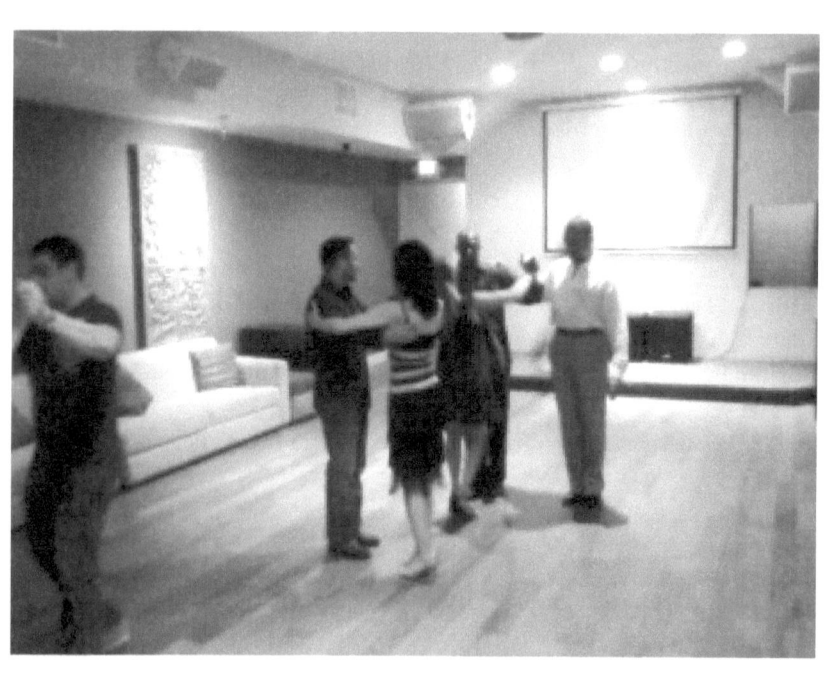

Sacred Hidden Thoughts continued

Three other Fascinating Artists: The Rubell Family Collection (RFC) is one of the leading collections of the contemporary art in the world. Starting in 1964, soon after Don and Mera Rubell were married, the collecting group expanded some years later when their children Jason and Jennifer, then quite young, joined their parents in buying and collecting art. They only show art they own. That is a founding principle of the Rubell Family Collection, a principle that gives them tremendous freedom and enormous constraints. The Rubell Family is passionately committed to the art and artists to which they respond. As art patrons first and foremost and as the heart and soul of an innovative collecting institution, the Rubells focus their efforts on acquiring a large body of work from a particular artist and conserving that work for future generations. They have a strong foundation of works by a core group of artists like Gary, Robert, and Henry.

It takes talent, natural ability, and the knowledge of the fundamentals of research study to be an artist like Gary Simmons, Henry Taylor, and Robert Colescott. Simmons searches and wants the new generation of today to believe that blacks are "people of an invented past, having lost connection to their tribes, names, customs of living and languages from Africa" (Riley 2007, 112). The question I am asking myself, did the architect of nature create Africa just for black people. Why do the artists relate all their works about blacks and that to the country of Africa? Are they talking about the importation and exploitation of black people to slavery, or are their thoughts about the differences between black people versus white people? Looking at their works and all the accumulated knowledge of arts they acquired, I have some sort of understanding that they believe everyone is made equal and should be treated fairly with respect and accept ourselves the way we are. "As with most serious artists, *Simmons* is a fine art printer for artists" (Riley 2007, 112). During my trip, I was thinking about his painting *Hollywood wherein* the artist is comparing white people as a letter in the alphabet using white color. The bottom of the painting shows the origination of people from earth and how they are disappearing to nowhere into the sky (*Duck, Duck, Noose* 1992). Simmons is teaching us the existence of human and what will happen to each and every one of us. A form of torture from the rope hanging in the poles shows how people in sin are creating their own death or maybe waiting in line for the last day. In *Erasure Series* (white-washed drawings) no. 2, 1992, Simmons is showing life after death, the process of reincarnation of people, how black turns to white, and white to black after this life.

Henry Taylor relates his story slightly different than Simmons. In his painting *Chicago Cook* (2008), Taylor is asking a question: do you get it? A picture of a mad lady is cooking her food in between housework; apparently, her servant did not show up for work that day. Looking at the street to see if the maid will come to work, the white lady does not know how to cook, expecting the maid to show up. The artist is trying to show how we need each other in our lives. What would happen to the employers without the help of their employees to do all the tasks that needed to be done? "Consequently, he approaches painting with reporter eyes, combined with a penetrating insight into the human condition" (Gray 2007, 1040).

Robert Colescott, in his painting *Modern Day Miracle* (1988), is showing the interaction of blacks with whites: an elderly white man dancing with a black lady or taking care of her whole family while every member of the family is happy and content eating, or cooking while enjoying and taking care of each other. Colescott tells a story about what he hopes should happen in this new society. Looking at America today shows a lot of hope for reunion, a big change people of all background and path in society have been dreaming about. In *Arabs: The Emir of Iswid (How the Gulf?)* (1992), the black were forced to slavery. Colescott reported black activists in different countries by the flags in his painting, which struck and fought for their freedom. He wants to remind us that the blacks deserve a better treatment. "Colescott engages art history and broad social allegory as starting points for surreal comedies of color and aesthetic improprieties" (Buuck 2008).

These three talented artists' works are very fascinating and inspiring to me, and I think they want everyone in search of unity to believe that history is past tense. Constant messages through painting of artists from all over the world showed almost the same story over and over again. It is an everlasting story in the soul of people of all generation that will remain. To the generation of today, history announces some sort of reconciliation among people of all color, class, and it is understandable that they are all of different ethnicity, just like they are all of different color and class.

The three artists share the same thoughts and are suffering for change toward love, sharing, caring, and applauding everyone's achievement in life. My question is who created black people black, it is not their color, it is not even their ancestors. Who created white people whites it is not even their color or ancestors either. Who had created mulattoe, it is not them or their ancestors. Some historians make us believe we are ugly or beautiful because of our ancestors. It is a divine question that originated from the creation of the whole universe; we are all searching for the right answer. Artists, musicians, dancers, designers, painters, as well as scientists from all over the world are continuously searching and inspiring, teaching the same stories. According to my dad (Professor Emmanuel L. Jacques), it had been set in the plans of God from the construction of the universe when God, the architect of nature, created everything that exists on earth. The artists cannot understand why people conceive things that way, why they want to prove that the whites need the blacks and the blacks need the whites . . . who were more intellectual than the blacks at the time of importation, but now it is different. It was a great learning experience and opportunity for me to visit the Rubell Family Collection in Miami (RFC).

Works Cited

Buuck, David. "*Robert Colescott* at Meridian Gallery." *Artweek* 39.1 (2008): 12-13. OmniFile Full Text Select. H. W. Wilson. The Art Institute of Fort Lauderdale 7 Aug. 2009 <http://vnweb.hwwilsonweb.com/.

Gray, Emma. "Oh Brother: *Henry Taylor*." *Art Review* (London, England) Apr. 2007: 40. OmniFile Full Text Select. H. W. Wilson. The Art Institute of Fort Lauderdale 7 Aug. 2009 <http://vnweb.hwwilsonweb.com/.

"*Henry* Fitch *Taylor*, A Surprising Modernist." *Antiques & Collecting Magazine* 110.7 (2005): 11. OmniFile Full Text Select. H. W. Wilson. The Art Institute of Fort Lauderdale 7 Aug. 2009 <http://vnweb.hwwilsonweb.com/.

Lankford, E. Louis, Kelly A. Scheffer, and Barbara Decker. "Quest and Questions: Learning in Our Time." *Art Education* 56.1 (2003): 25-32. OmniFile Full Text Select. H. W. Wilson. The Art Institute of Fort Lauderdale 7 Aug. 2009 <http://vnweb.hwwilsonweb.com/.

Riley, Cheryl R. "*Gary Simmons*: The Art of Erasure." *Ebony* 62.6 (2007): 108110, 112. OmniFile Full Text Select. H. W. Wilson. The Art Institute of Fort Lauderdale 7 Aug. 2009 <http://vnweb.hwwilsonweb.com/.

Valdez, Sarah. "*Robert Colescott* at Kravets/Wehby." *Art in America* 95.3 (2007): 171-2. OmniFile Full Text Select. H. W. Wilson. The Art Institute of Fort Lauderdale 7 Aug. 2009 <http://vnweb.hwwilsonweb.com/.

Lack of communication between people of the same race as well as different ethnicities, can cause the entire destruction of a country. We know communication is an important part of preventing violence, war, divorce in established families, killing, kidnapping, just to name a few. This is probably the reason for the serious decline in civilization today. Good communication on the other hand, promotes friendship, respect and acceptation for others, better understanding of the world setting and business partnership and helps in the creation of a better society. Also lack of communication isolates people, creating misunderstanding and lack of trust between them. Therefore, they will never be able to work toward a common goal.

The problem in society today seems to be an unsolved story. Society throughout the world is increasingly interconnected. The great increasing of racial and cultural diversity should bring balance to the society around us. In an increasing interconnected world we tend to understand ourselves only to the extent that we understand and accept others. Sociology invites us to learn new ways of looking at the world around us. Sociological perspective helps us access the truth of common sense.

There are three ways of communication people all over the world should use to communicate between themselves. We have a developed an ability to learn to the highest level possible the skill of writing and oral communication however, we do not pay enough attention to movement in dance. In reference to writing we learn how to combine letters in different languages, we learn to speak and understand music construction and gestures. But, no attention is paid to etiquettes of body language in different dance art form. There are universities in every country in the world the youth can go to earn a degree in musicology. The schools for Choreology are limited and not funded. Music and Dance are two Universal language of the world, a gift from God to his people as part of communication.

Sociological perspective empowers us to be active participants in our society. The better we understand how society operates, the more effective citizens we become. As C. Wright Mills Explained: It is the sociological perspective that turns a private problem into a public issue. As we come to see, how society affects our life, we may decide to support it as it is, or we may set out with others to change it.

In the United States, the written and spoken language used to communicate is English and the music or dance traditional art forms are swing, lindy-hop, fox-trot etc . . . Not many young adults in this country are interested in learning the American traditions. In ways people interact there is something lacking. A simple gesture may lead to a fight. It is very difficult for the less fortunate to interact with the rest of the teens when it comes to Socialization. It is even worse for a non-English speaking immigrant. In my opinion they develop a feeling of insecurity, inequality and lack of acceptance.

As a natural progression of tradition and cultural mores, no one needs to go to school to speak a native language as it is the case for music and dance. How many musicians are playing music without going to school to learn how music is constructed? And how many dance teachers today are teaching without a dance teacher's certification? The answers are many enough to damage people's physical and mental wellbeing. The majority of these musicians and dance teachers developed a lack of discipline and respect which they pass on to their students. The multicultural study of the basic understanding of the foundation of music and dance presents a distinctive opportunity to enhance and enrich our understanding of communication with others.

Questionnaire:

1) How can we explain the paradox, there are universities all over the world for musicology, whereas there are enough for choreology?

2) Why is it important for people to learn the basics of different traditional dance art form?

3) Do you think the government (City officials) should refuse to issue a license to dance teachers without certification to open Dance Studio?

4) What is the danger of learning to dance from non-qualified teachers?

5) What is the main problem of dancing off timing to music?

Social experience is the basic of personality. The family affects socialization in many ways. For me it is the most important socializing agent of all. I came from a family of twelve children. My dad was working with the board of education in my country. My mom was a housewife taking care of all of us doing the cooking, cleaning, laundry and sewing etc . . . with little help.

My dad's primary occupation was to organize public schools in different cities in our state or what we can call department. Every two years the family had to relocate to where ever the construction was being done. He took time during the construction of the school building to train teachers who would be responsible for following the curriculum and directing the school. When this was done; he had to move on to the next construction. During all those years past, I was surrounded with people from different classes of life.

My schooling was done at home until the age of twelve. There were at that time 6 children in the family, we all grew up the same way. Since I was educated at home, I was never among my peers. It was challenging for me to interact and develop friendships with children my own age. It was a great learning experience and unique. I must say, I will never forget my mom was our first teacher, for reading, writing and social skills. Some of my daily activities: breakfast in the morning, learning to write words hundreds of times, reading them loudly with perfect pronunciation etc.

On weekends, my mom would take me to folk dance lessons. As it was at that time the only cultural activity in the city. It was organized as a networking program to meet people. My dad was never there during the daytime. He wanted to make sure we all learned something, and so, he added his own assignment for the next day, asking my mom to follow up. As schooling is critical for obtaining the knowledge and skills needed for adult roles, the social life of the family has been shown to have a considerable bearing upon the values and orientations children learn.

Man alone is capable of making sense of what he sees, around him by using symbols to organize his thoughts and communicate his observations. The unique form of communication between human beings is the spoken language. Other species make use of sounds, smells and gestures.

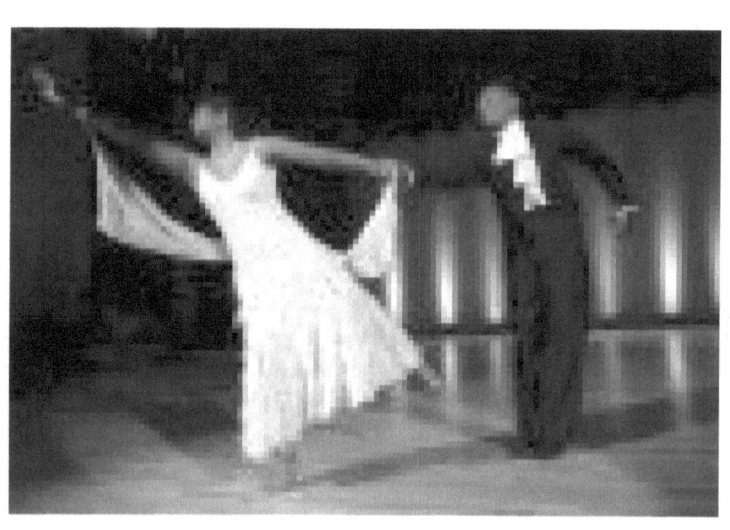

Today's culture generally represents nations, each with its own cultural identity. Based on my observation, the Cuban Community cares more about their own norms than any other ethnic communities. They organize together to conserve and promote their language, music and dance art forms to communicate with the rest of the people around them. Some of them have no interest in learning the English language they create their own social control. Unlike some other communities for example the Haitians believe, that if you live in the United States you should learn the language and the customs of the country. They do not have enough interest in promoting their cultural norms. They are more interested in learning the English, French and Spanish languages than the Creole. Norms are the rules or expectations with which people orient their behaviors and govern themselves. Adopting certain values, learning others way of living leads people to be more divers in society.

When it comes to cultural activities the Haitians with higher education are proud and enjoy the fact that they are diverse. It has to be something important enough in their culture for them to fight and work for. As it is, they are willing to give up something of their own in exchange for different values.

Let's not wait though

Martin Barthold, a Haitian ballroom dance instructor, is a fellow brother of mine. He was very instrumental in the construction of the New Millennium Ballroom in Florida. I was surprised to meet a young fellow ballroom dancer from Haiti, the country of my birth, with such a soul similar as mine. As he mentions in his poetry book, "Let's change the face of this planet now. Let's give it a full makeover—Not a surgical one but, a spiritual one, the kind that changes the interior, not the exterior. Let's change the heart of the planet. Let's make a change that can free the soul, open the eyes upon a new dimension of life, and bring us all together in harmony, unity, and compassion for others. (2010-Symphony of love P-63, Haiti earthquake relief printing)."

I knew there will be hope for the future of Haiti. As I mentioned before, the generation of today needs to set an example to properly manage the help we are getting from the USA and the international communities. We cannot let it get into the wrong hands. I have never experienced what happened in 1986, I was very fortunate to be in the USA, since 1984. Knowing what Haiti was during Papa Doc's era, in general the government was more powerful and the army was formed with the most educated individual's in a decade. Unfortunately Papa Doc did not finish organizing his social democracy.

1971 marked the downfall of the Pearl of the Caribbean when Baby Doc took over the presidency. He was too weak to handle all the works left by his father. A constant traffic of boats entered Miami, causing a decline of our identity and our agricultural forces. The old silly tactic poor poorer, rich richer, resurfaced the Island. It is not surprising then, that the generation under fifty today does not remember. They feel those who do know (people over seventy-five) are too old to even put their noses into what is not their business.

Martin a well-educated dance teacher, witnessed in 1986, the liberation of Haiti: as he said, "My soul country, I was there during the downfall of Papa Doc, I had followed the procession, I sang with them the song of deliverance. I saw many decapilation of so-called "tonton macoute". In Haiti, we pray to be alive. There is no safe place, nowhere to run, no 911 call to help. Kids, teenagers, adults as well as seniors are all in the mercy of God". I can consider myself lucky for not being there at that time. However I did feel their pain.

Earthquake

On January 12, 2010 an unpredictable tragedy in a form of an earthquake killed many people and caused more of us to suffer. We have to understand God the creator of all has a plan for everything. We all need to learn and prove to our international friends that we are able to use the help to rebuild Haiti to the highest possible standard: new ports, new roads, power lights in every city, new factories, schools and clean beaches to attract more tourists. We need to educate our kids to stay home. In addition to build grand hotel ballrooms to help in the exchange of our cultural arts form. This is to me all we have to give back to our overseas friends who cared enough to help in the reorganization of this country. Some people develop or simply learn a weird customized behavior that seems to be impossible to exchange with the rest of the world. If we can come up with new concepts in ways of thinking and do business at a universal standard, then and only then, our behaviors will change for the better.

TANGO BEFORE BREAKFAST

(Screenplay: Healing From Dancing)

Logline:

A Television reporter takes a chance on life and champions self hate and defies the odds of success by abandoning his job, money and lavish possessions to fall in love with a new found hobby (Ballroom Dancing) that ultimately changes his life and the lives of all who comes in contact with it.

Brief mini-synopsis

The wealthy reporter learns the price of peace over power as he finds that the story he would one day cover, would be that of his own. He champions self deprivation, job dissatisfaction and bureaucratic imprisonment upon discovering a new found hobby (tango) that would not only change his life and all that come in contact with it, but ultimately the world. What was once a hobby becomes a remedy for change? Theme:" Dancing, a therapeutic art, with the power to change"

TANGO BEFORE BREAKFAST
(Healing From dancing) Based on a True Story!

A graduate from AIFL School of Journalism and broadcasting, a professional Soccer player, employee at a television station, Michel, a seemingly abundant 36 years old man could call himself lucky. With a humanitarian as father who serves in high ranks in government, Michel's lavish possesions and a zesty educated respected technologist as a girlfriend, Michel would seem to have all that a man of his stature would die for.

Driven by his dissatisfaction of the bureaucracy associated with the political realm, and his insatiable appetite for change, Michel searches for a career that would fill the void and finds it in tango before breakfast.

This experiment takes a dramatic turn when he discovers that this phenomenon is life changing. Eager to embody the spirit of his father, he seeks to learn the art, only to find that he must proceed with caution because the wrong move could cost him his life.

While pushing his mission, he joins forces with his father and proposes to start schools for dancing in an effort to introduce the concept of "tango the spirit of change". His father adopts the notion and decides to use it as a conduit through which he could help promote and expand the law for no smoking in the night clubs.

Political figures driven by envy, hears about this and fear the drastic change would cost them, so the devise a plan to blackball Michel's dance school and ban it from ever opening. Michel finds himself back in the previous position and leans on the love of his life to help pull him through. Time runs rapid as Michel and his lover are challenged by their oppressors to undermine the art form.

They will have to work around the clock to beat their opponents at

their own game. The two will put together a dance, health, weight loss and fitness studio in an effort to spread change by bringing awareness to this art via an international tour in order to expose the faultiness in the crooked political arena and to bring change to a dying generation.

TANGO BEFORE BREAKFAST:
(Healing From dancing)

Opening: SCENRY FILM (TO BEGIN)
WITH GOD FIRST CREATION,(SKY/EARTH FOOTAGE,
with A COUPLE, Ballet Dancing warm up.

EARLY MORNING NEWSPAPER MAN IS DELIVERING MAIL, MICHEL IS SEEN SLEEPING AT HOME. MICHEL IS SEEN IN HIS BED COVERED W/PILLOWS/ BLANKET SLEEPING. THE ALARM CLOCK WAKES HIM UP. HE IS HARD TO GET UP. FINALLY HE WALKS TO THE BATHROOM LOOKS IN THE MIRROR, PICKS UP THE SHAVING CREAM. THE TANGO MUSIC STARTS PLAYING (SURPRISES HIM) HE LOOKS BEHIND (NO BODY'S THERE) AT THE SAME TIME, INSIDE THE BATHROOM THE WATER NOISE ADDED TO THE MUSIC.

A LADY'S HAND (LONG NAILS) IS SEEN AT THE DOOR, ENTERS THE BATHROOM. HE TANGO WALKS TO THE SHOWER (NO LADY THERE) TAKES A SHOWER HIMSELF.(WITH ASTONISHMENT)

Michel dresses to work, picks up the newspaper in the mail. Is seen inside the News room of channel 105 news. conference table 12 colleagues (journalists) are making plans about what news to report. Michel Said nothing making a face.

TERESSA IS SEEN AT A RESTAURANT EARLY EVENING ALONE, HEART BROKEN. WAITRESS BRING HER A GLASS OF WINE. A GOOD FRIEND LOUIS WALK IN, SURPRISE TO SEE HER, TERESSA DROP THE WINE GLASS CRYING OVER THE BREAK UP WITH HER BOYFRIEND.

LOUIS (a friend walk in)
When is the break up?

TERESSA
About eight month ago

LOUIS
How did the romance happen?

TERESSA
Sweat me off my feet

LOUIS
How did that Happen

TERESSA
I don't Know, you're going out for
business, woo there it is.

LOUIS
HaHAHa! Mr. right. (laughing)

TERESSA
OH . . . Yes, he send me flowers for no
reason, the romantic diner, late
night calls for hours and all the
special attentions.

LOUIS
And then, what?

TERESSA
I felt he is pulling away.

LOUIS
How did you handle this?

TERESSA
Well at first I blame myself;
Then I cried, then called every person
I know to discuss it and, after 14.000 calls . . .

LOUIS
Hey, wait a minute, are you sure he
was pulling away, what was the sign?

TERESSA
Well, the phone call was not this
frequent. when we're together he
seems to be preoccupy and, stop
paying attention to my life.

LOUIS
So, what did you do?

TERESSA
I threw myself into his life, his
career, his family and, to a point I
wasn't even known who I was anymore.
I hated myself but, I couldn't stop myself.

LOUIS
But, ultimately you did, you left.

TERESSA
Right! . . .

LOUIS
How you are able to do it?

TERESSA (singing)
I had this dream,,, I had this dream
that I had to fulfill one day . . .
(song take the risk)

TERESSA IS SEEN AT A BEAUTIFUL RESTAURANT SETTING IN A LIVE
ORCHESTRA: SINGING A BEAUTIFUL SONG (TAKE THE RISK SLOW WALTZ)
BALLROOM DANCERS ON THE FLOOR DANCING TO THE SONG.

The next day. At the other end Michel, at home Watching bad morning news . . .
ready to go to work . . . rushing to his car at his boss office . . . Slams the door . . .
staff are scared he will end up in a quarrel.

                    MICHEL
            What's going on, are you still doing
            it. What's wrong about telling the
                truth? it is not right. the
                    youth . . .

                ALAN (WALK IN)
            I was ready to air your story
            Michel. It makes better sense to
            tell the truth. I am against make up
                    stories.

                ALTON (THE PRESIDENT)
            wait a minute, who is paying my
            bills! I understand how you feel, I
            have to make the payroll, including
                the mortgage here.

                MICHEL (W/AN UGLY LOOK}
            Mr. Alton, it's still not right to
            mislead the public. our job is to
            educate, we are train to provide the
            right cast for the next generation
            to follow, as Michel slams the
            door . . . this is not where I should be.

Michel is seen in his car 40mph in the parking garage driving away passing a big bus
on the hwy. is seen packing, at his house . . . walking in the front door. He goes to
wash his face (washroom)

                MICHEL (walking in the living room)
                I cannot understand, the whole
                    world feels up w/evils. It's
                like . . . it looks like, night club (hip-hops)

business. Lord, lords please help me . . .

(KNEE DOWN) THEN PICK UP THE NEWSPAPER) STARTS READING.

TOOK A SHOWER, HE IS SEEN DRESSED AT THE CANADIAN BALLROOM CLUB . . . DANCING WITH THE SENIORS . . . TERESSA IS SEEN AT THE CORNER OF THE ROOM OVER LOOKING AT HIM. HE LOOKS AT HER ENVISION A BEAUTIFUL TANGO CHOREOGRAPHY SHOW WITH HER . . . BOTH ARE SEEN IN A DEEP CONVERSATION AT A TABLE . . . MANY SENIOR DANCING IN THE BACKGROUND . . . AT THE END. THE ROOM IS EMPTY . . . THE COUPLE LEFT ALONE ARE SEEN HAPPY HUGGING IN THE MIDDLE OF THE DANCE FLOOR. THEN IN AN EMPTY PARKING LOT KISSING GOODBYE.

TERESSA (DRIVING HOME) V. O
I feel healed, this is my dream man.
He can dance Wow.

Teresa is walking at her apartment, in Bed watching a Ballroom dance instructional video.

V. O
Healing from a broken heart is a
difficult and a private process, No
matter who is responsible for ending
a loving relationship, you
experience tremendous pains,
resentment and sorrow-These emotions
must be recognized and dealt with in
order to have another healthy
relationship.

(TERESSA (MAKING A PHONE CALL).
Hi! it is me, did you get home safe?

MICHEL
Oh yes, I am glad you care, What are
you doing?

TERESSA
Learning Ballroom dancing,

MICHEL
you are kidding . . .

TERESSA

No . . . on TV . . . a gift DVD I got from
my parent a while ago . . . You make me
fall in love with dancing . . .

MICHEL

Dancing since I was little is in my
blood. I learn from Arthur Murray
studio.

TERESSA

I know you are tired, Good night my
dear . . .

MICHEL

Good night my dear. see you
tomorrow.

TERESSA

Good night love . . . see you tomorrow.

EARLY MORNING, MICHEL CALL THE OFFICE, HIS BOSS ON THE LINE

MICHEL

Mr. Alton, I am not coming back,
Just to let you know . . .

ALTON

What! you! are you out of mind? you
think this fucking Dancing will make
you fortune, hey . . .

MICHEL

I do not need your job! do not worry
about me.

ALTON

Get the fuck out there, go to dance,
dance . . .

Michel Hangs up. is seen at the soccer field playing soccer at a big stadium . . . Then
at home. Opening the front door for Teresa, who is very happy comfortable with

her dream man. she goes outside in the back yard a beautiful garden. Michel does not seem happy, watching The news. His girl friend comes out the back yard to the kitchen w/ fruits . . .

TERESSA
Cheri! are you here What's
happening? You are not happy, You
are not working today.

MICHEL
Did you see the news, they twisted
my reports, it's all lies.

TERESSA
Cheri, you need to look at it as a
job. we know it is not fair to the
general public. I brings you some
fruits.

MICHEL
It is incredible, making fortune by
mislead people and the future
generation will be very confused.

TERESSA
The future generation is in danger.
The young generation is out of hand
because of what happening, People only Need to
entertainment, ent. only.

MICHEL
Education is power, future of a
Country . . . any nation depends on the
kids you are preparing today.

IN N. Y, MICHEL FATHER, THE STATE GOVERNOR AT HOME TALKING TO HIS COLLEAGUE IN FLORIDA OVER THE PHONE.

N. Y GOVERNOR (PHONE)
We can't cross our arm and let them
do whatever they want.

FLORIDA GOVERNOR (PHONE)
The law is already passed. no
Smoking inside clubs, restaurant and
bars . . . no under age in club that has
liquor license.

N. Y GOVERNOR
What about the media people
Christ . . . it's all B. S . . .

FLORIDA GOVERNOR
We are working on that . . . I am
looking forward to meeting you next
week.

N. Y GOVERNOR
I will arrive, Miami airport at
2pm . . . You take care . . .

MICHEL AND TERESSA AT THE DINING TABLE, MICHEL APPARTMENT
EVENING TIME, GOOD FOOD, OVER A GLASS OF WINE . . . TERESSA IS AN
EXCELLENT COOK.

TERESSA
What are you going to do now. If you
quit the TV Station. (massaging his
neck)

MICHEL
It's alright, I do have enough,,, I
need to take a break from all those
bullshit. I will continue on my
research.

TERESSA
You are a dreamer, It will be
alright. research something you love
doing, something that can serve as
an inspiring; some sort of
stimulating ART like dancing, music.

MICHEL
Something to teach everybody how to
be fair to each others. something I
Enjoy doing and still use it to make
a good living.

TERESSA
What will it be?

MICHEL
The Origin of Music And Dance!

TERESSA
There you go! you are a good
dreamer. Good night, my dear!
(Hugging)

Teresa is seen living the house front door in her Lexus . . . backs off the parking lot.
Michel eyes close at the dining table is dreaming . . . A view of kid's Ballroom dance
competition in Blackpool England. Then He is performing a beautiful Vienna waltz.
Back to normal, gets up the chair goes to his bedroom, takes a shower, is seen in bed
watching TV falls asleep alone.

AT THE AIRPORT MICHEL PICKS UP HIS FATHER (EMMANUEL) IS SEEN WITH
BOTH GOVERNORS IN MIAMI AIRPORT.

THEY DO NOT SEE EACH OTHER OFTEN, THEY ALL HAVE A FANCY DINNER
PARTY MEETING WHERE TERESSA AND MICHEL WERE AT DINING TABLE
OVER LISTEN TO ALL THE POLITICAL CHANGES TO BE MADE.

GOVERNOR FLORIDA (TYLER)
Ladies/Gentlemen: In honor of my
friend/colleague Governor of N. Y
(Mr. Emmanuel) welcome to our diner,
Bon appétit.

GOVERNOR N. Y (MR. EMMANUEL)
It's been a pleasure to be here in
Florida, Thank you all, Bon appétit.

DURING THE COCKTAIL/DISCUSSIONS, MICHEL OVER HEARD THE
CONVERSATION, REVEALS HIS DECISION TO BECOME A BALLROOM DANCE

EDUCATOR TO HELP INTO THE DEVELOPMENT OF ALL FORM OF DANCE IN THE SCHOOL SYSTEM STARTING FROM ELEMENTARY SCHOOL, AND TO THE CREATION OF A MULTICULTURAL CLUB IN SOUTH FLORIDA, WITH PURPOSE IS TO BRING PEOPLE ALL OVER THE WORLD TOGETHER IN AN EXCHANGE OF THEIR OWN CULTURAL IDENTITY, A NEW CONCEPT IN THE WAY PEOPLE DANCE TO MUSIC.

4th of July independence day celebration, Michel at Teresa's family house with friends and relatives enjoying each others company comes true with his words, his trip to London tomorrow. Everybody convince Teresa that it is the right decision. Michel quietly pulls himself out of the party. Later on, he reveals to his friends that he is considering taking his relationship w/Teresa to the next level.

EARLY MORNING MICHEL IN THE ROOM PACKING HIS LUGGAGE FOR THE TRIP. IS SEEN ON THE ROAD TO THE AIRPORT . . . AT THE AIRPORT LOTS, IS WALKING, DIALS A # OVER THE PHONE W/ TERESSA.

Michel
Hi! I am on my way to London. I
left my car at Miami airport, lot
dolphin 5 floor Fj6 . . . Have someone
move it home . . . you have the
key . . . I'll see you when I get back.

TERESSA
For how long, you run away Just like
that.(V. O) what is the hurry?

MICHEL
There is a 2 years Program for Dance
Educator at the institute of
Choreology . . . I may have to stay for
a while. Everything will be fine.

AIRPLANE TAKES OFF: MICHEL IS SEEN IN LONDON, WALKING, BEAUTIFUL VIEW OF LONDON BRIDGE . . . ENTERING INSTITUTE OF CHOREOLOGY, REGISTERING FOR DANCE TEACHERS TRAINING PROGRAMS. SECRETARY DIRECTS MICHEL TO THE PRINCIPAL OFFICE.

MRS. BENNETH (SCHOOL PRINCIPAL)
Have a seat gentleman, The first
year of your learning will be the

Psychology of teaching and some
study of human body alignment . . .

MICHEL
Why I have to study psychology?
dancing has nothing to do with that.

MRS. BENNETH
Since Dancing, first has a lot to do
with your Brain and joints in your
Body, we need to develop the skill
of the communication process in our
body. Choreology is the equivalent
of musicology, A misinterpretation
of music through body movement
creates a disorientation of the
brain settings. Dancing teachers
need to know how it work. Specially
when it come to teaching young
students to dance.

MICHEL
OUWAOU! I understand there are lots
of emotional feeling to develop
through dancing. I never Know that
dancing is part of medicine. I love
it, I cannot wait.

MRS. BENNETH
Very well! Welcome to the Institute.

MICHEL
University of boogie, I love it. I am
a journalist.

MRS. BENNETH
Great! Here is, all you need to go
over for Class next week, I will see
you in class congratulations and
welcome.

Michel is in London walking, a view of London tourist attraction . . . pigeons fly away. Meets with Veronica on the street. Bang to each other. Michel falls on the ground.

VERONICA (LOOKS SURPRISE)
Excuse me! I am so sorry sir.

MICHEL
No, no That's alright . . . Never mind.

VERONICA
Are you from here, but . . . you having an accent

MICHEL
Not from here really! I am
American . . . where are you from?

VERONICA
Chinese/American.

MICHEL
Wonderful combination, do you live here?

BOTH ARE SEEN WALKING ALONG THE WATERWAYS

Veronica
I live in LA with my parent, I am
here visiting. I will move to
Florida, for my allergy . . .

MICHEL
I do live in Florida . . .

VERONICA
Interesting, I will be living in
Davie In my parent's home.

MICHEL
you are Next to me, I live in
Hallandale . . .

VERONICA
Great I am here for the Ballroom

dance competition . . . I am going to
Blackpool tomorrow just to watch.

MICHEL
Woo! Blackpool, that's where the world
top competitors compete.

VERONICA
The whole week in blackpool, my dad
wanted me to learn Ballroom dancing
I do have Ballet training Though.

MICHEL
Lovely . . . I want to be a Ballroom
Dance educator . . .

VERONICA
I will look for you in Blackpool.

MICHEL
I will be there looking for you too.

MICHEL, is seen in a train, then walks by himself at the sea side in BLACKPOOL, LONDON, the road is pave. lots of attractions, people are walking on the street, car, taxi, transportation buses, train are passing by. The whole City is seen far in the distance. Lots of activities

MICHEL (V. O)
Our hearts is so often
burst with the fullness of treasured
moment in time as . . . we continue on
this exiting journey called life, to
stop often and realize that god
creates each of us with everything
within to be happy and content. To
be capable of inner wisdom in giving
and receiving unconditionally, to
count our blessing in every lovely
sight to see. In the music from high
to low what . . . leads the body to move
& dance and becomes an inspiration
toward keeping a healthy body and

soul. Dancing has been a connecting
golden thread between people of all
countries. dance has continued to
nourish our soul in the direction of
happiness, good health, faith and
serenity. There is always and
forever the joy of the music and
dance.

A group of dancers performing a great piece of choreography

(fade to Michel in his room desk writing/reading.

Veronica is seen browsing in London . . . In a formal attire Michel is seen in a taxi:
Veronica outside the winter garden resort waiting. couple walking in winter garden
Blackpool . . . to a Ballroom Dance competition . . . same as the dream Michel had.

VERONICA
That is where I want to be. They are
wonderful dancers. it' s very
inspiring.

MICHEL
Extravaganza! this is the most
attractive Ballroom in the world.
Winter Garden. Look at this couple,
Every country is being represented.

MC (V. O)
From Italy couple # 23 from Germany
Couple # 44, From USA couple # 12
From China couple # 14, from England
couple # 18, from,,,,,,,

BALLET/BALLROOM DANCE STUDIO, MICHEL ENTERS READY TO WARM
UP . . . ABOUT 1/2 A DOZEN YOUNG COUPLE IN TRAINING. CLASS ROOM
SETTING,,, TRAINEES ARE TAKING NOTES.

MRS. BENNETH
What are the five Basic elements of
music Dancers should know to dance
properly.

YOUNG GIRL/MAN (CHARACTER FUNNY)
1) Rhythm 2) Tempo 3) Beats Value)
4) B. P. M/M. P. M 5) High & Low . . .

The whole class is seen moving to a grand ballroom floor

MRS. BENNETH
Very good. Let' s start with cha cha
cha . . . warming up together w/
music . . .

A SCENE WHERE MRS BENNETH ASKING EACH ONE TO DEMONSTRATE A
COMBINATION STEP ACCORDING TO MUSIC.

COUPLE#1
Dancing the Dance pattern . . .

MRS. BENNETH
NO. NO. NOoo. (2&3&4&1) the cha cha
cha . . . stands for 4&1,,, it is the
time you have to go (side closed
side . . .) next Couple . . .

COUPLE # 2
Dancing same pattern w/ music this
time accordingly . . .

MRS. BENNETH
yes. yes's . . . Let's move to
waltz . . . the only music w/3 main
beats in a bar, it's a 3/4 time.

COUPLE #3
Dancing a pattern (fairly well)

MRS. BENNETH (SERIOUSLY LAUGH)
To create the true characteristic of
the waltz we need to lower at the
end of the 3rd beat of the music,
step on 1 and start rise at the end
of 1 continuously on 2 up to 3 . . . and
lower . . .(She demonstrates)

All couple in front of big mirror practicing timing to a beautiful Rumba music. Mrs. Benneth Call Michel to the office, then are seen walking on the street and then in a park walking together . . .

MRS. BENNETH (V. O)
There are as many type of rhythm as
there are cultures in the
world . . . Choreographers in Ballroom
tend to be able to identify and
understanding the Basic Foundation
of each one of them . . . with proper
notations . . . the graphic design of
every movement, with music is
exactly what choreology is . . .

MICHEL
It is not quit a universal language.

MRS. BENNETH
It is, communication between our
bio-rhythm with rhythm within music
translate through our body.

MICHEL
I am very Excited to be here, I
want to be one of the top.

MRS. BENNETH
I am sure you will . . . Dancers from
all over the world come to Study
here.

MICHEL IS SEEN GOING INTO THE HOTEL. ON THE COMPUTER DOING RESEARCH STUDY . . .

TWO YEARS LATER
GRAND DINER GALA IN CELEBRATION OF THE DANCE TEACHER GRADUATION. IN BANQUET SET-UP. MICHEL RECIEVES DIPLOMA AS A CHOREOLOGIST. LOTS OF PICTURES TAKING, WITH HIS GUEST VERONICA AND COLLEAGUE GRADUATES.

A VIEW OF MICHEL IN HIS ROOM, THEN IN LONDON TAXI CAB GOING TO
THE AIRPORT.

MICHEL IN MIAMI TAXI GOING HOME,,, ENTER HIS APARTMENT, NORMAL
LIFE . . . AND TERESSA WALK IN, VERY SURPRISE HAPPY TO SEE MICHEL. BIG
WELCOME HOME CELEBRATION TERESSA IS COOKING DINNER . . . AT THE
DINING TABLE. TERESSA'S FAMILY MEMBERS WALK IN.(SURPRISE PARTY)
WELCOME MICHEL BACK . . . ALL DECIDE TO OPEN GRAND BALLROOM IN
FLORIDA.

MICHEL
I finally find what is best for me.
The most attractive ballroom dance
club, that will bring people all
over the world together, a dream
come true, Teresa.

TERESSA
You're phenomenon, there is an empty
space next to Publix plaza in
Hallandale . . . back of Morrison
Cafeteria.

MRS. CAPLAN
Michel deserves his own studio. I
believe it this plaza runs by
Investment Management & Associates.

MICHEL
We will be able to set it up as the
first Multicultural Dance club
organization. To attract the youth
to Dance Ballroom we, need to have a
liquor license.

MR. CAPLAN
What a great concept, A Ballroom
dance Studio/Night club. non-Smoking
Club.

I. M. A realtor Ronald Pierre at a restaurant making up a

lease agreement on the facility . . . Dance Creation Ballroom
Inc.

MICHEL

Ron I need a lease for 15 years with
option to Buy. Ballroom w/liquor is
a new concept that will take us at
least 10 years to promote worldwide,
We are not going to make money right
away. We need to create a good name
first . . .

RONALD

You get 5 years with 2 renewal
options. The first 6 months is free
for demolition & renovation, and
city regulations.

MICHEL

It's a lot of money, to demolish and
remodel the place.

RONALD

We will replace the a/c units, or
you can replace them in exchange for
free rent . . .(shake hands) the
lease will be ready on Monday.

MICHEL

we will stop by your office with the
deposit to finalize. Thank you Ronald.

Michel at the contractor office, making appointment to come to the location for
estimation.

Michel, Teresa and Mrs. Kaplan. Then in a car going home.

CONTRACTOR AT HOME W/WIFE, TALKING HOW THEY WILL DOUBLE THE
COST OF CONSTRUCTION. CONTRACTOR HAS NO STATE LICENSE.
JERRY (CONTRACTOR AT THE BUILDING SITE)
The whole work will cost about $85.000.00.

MICHEL
How long will it takes to finish?

JERRY
5 to 8 weeks., You will be ready to
the grand opening . . .

MICHEL
Let's go for it. You have a deal.

A PICTURE VIEW OF AN EMPTY ROOM, DEMOLISH WITH JANET THE
SECRETARY AND MICHEL LOOKING AT HOW TO DESIGN THE INTERIOR.
MICHEL PHONE RINGS. IT'S TERESSA.

TERESSA (AT HOME)
My friend, What if you call it: The
Millennium Ballroom. It would be a
great name, to open the Ballroom at
the millennium, Dec 1999.

MICHEL
Why not, you are inspired by god to
find a name like this Terra.

TERESSA
I know you will turn it into a mango
tree.

MICHEL ON THE COMPUTER REGISTERING THE NAME MILLENNIUM
BALLROOM INC. THE NEXT DAY TERESSA, KNOCK AT MICHEL APARTMENT
DOOR . . . MICHEL IN PIJAMAS OPEN THE DOOR.

MICHEL
Hey! teerybell! Come in, it is your
home.

TERESSA
I know Dr. knight! I am moving to
Clearwater to help my Dad with his
business . . .

Michel
What? I cannot manage without you.
you are the only one who knows
how . . . I can only teach Dancing.

TERESSA
I will be there for The MC. at the
grand opening, I will always be
there to help any time I can.

MICHEL
It's not going to be easy for me to
run all this without you.

NEXT DAY AT Goldcoast Ballroom a group of people are gossiping, some are excited,
cannot wait for the grand opening . . .

Michel Struggles with landlord management, city official to get license, and building
contractors.

CITY INSPECTOR
I cannot approve this
license . . . this is a list of what you
need to do to be in city code. You
need to hire a license contractor,
this Jerry is not a State
license . . . Good luck.

MICHEL
What? contractor is not license
w/the State.

INSPECTOR
At the city hall, they will give you
a list of License contractor you can
choose from . . . one for fire
sprinkler, plumbing and electrical.
Everything has to be redone to pass
your inspection . . . (living seriously
to the parking lot).

SIX MONTH LATER DEC 31, 1999, MILLENNIUM BALLROOM IN HALLANDALE . . .
GRAND OPENING OF A UNIQUE MULTICULTURAL DANCE CLUB ORG . . . GALA
PARTY. PEOPLE FROM ALL OVER THE WORLD IS THERE TO CELEBRATE . . .

TERESSA (M. C)
Speech . . .
. . . Terry
announces Michel & partner on the
dance floor.
Michel and partner 5 Ballroom Dance performances with
beautiful Costumes. the whole public applauds.

TERESSA
At this time I am turning the Mic to
the one and only, the infamous.
Michel . . .

MICHEL
Thank you Terra: Michel delivers
Speech . . .

(. . . AND DANCE PARTY CONTINUE)
. . .
During the party Jack Feldman, a short nasty evil man, very jealous confronted Michel
while leaving the party.

JACK
You don't belong here, One day you
will have to pay to get in this
door. This place will belong to me.

MICHEL
It's for sell, How are you going to
own it? red neck. it's too classy
for you. no-Smoking, it's a Christian
Club.

JACK
We will see!

Take (to a dance Piece, explain jealousy through motion.

MICHEL & TERESSA, AT THE MALL SHOPPING, EMELINE AND HUSBAND AT
THE MALL (LOOKING HAPPY WITH EACH OTHER) THEN MEET MICHEL &
TERESSA, THEY KNEW EACH OTHERS . . .

MR. PETER
I am so sorry I was not able to
attend the grand opening . . . Emeline
and I Will come very often.

EMELINE
I heard it the most attractive
Ballroom in south Florida.

TERESSA
Yes, It is. It was a nightmare
$350.000.00 in remodeling the Place.
I do hope Ballroom Dancers will
appreciate it and support the
effort.

EMELINE
It a lot of money to invest. you
could own the facility with that
kind of cash.

MICHEL
I know . . . it's too late now. I will
make it back . . . we just need your
supports.

MR PETER
You can count on us

MICHEL AT THE STUDIO TEACHING TAMMY AND ANDY PRIVATE LESSON . . .
TERESSA AT THE OFFICE WORKING ON THE COMPUTER . . . MICHEL WALK
IN AFTER THE CLASS.

TERESSA
Oh! look you get an email from
CID/Unesco.

MICHEL

Ok! it is an invitation to the world
congress on dance research
study . . . an opportunity to showcase
our original works.

TERESSA

You wanted to create the Compas
dance . . . this is something you can
present to them. you will be the
author of the compas Dance art form.

MICHEL

That's a great idea, let's send an
Abstract paper to Mr. Raftis
Alkis,,, Dominique is moving to
port-au-prince, she can help in
Promoting this as a New concept of
Dance for the people.

TERESSA

It look very vulgar the way they
dance the Compas . . . beside the people
dance in the dark. Dance is a
national identity, the beauty of the
dance is missing.

MICHEL

Well, I want to send a message to
the board of education. if they can
make Ballroom dancing part of
education Starting from elementary
school, that will help create a
better identity, a better society.

TERESSA

I agree, what we see now in the
clubs will not be impossible to
change. no teacher can teach old dog
new trick . . . It has to Start with the
kids.

MICHEL TAKE THE OFFICE CHAIR, TERRY GETS UP GOES TO THE
RESTROOM . . . MICHEL CONTINUE TYPING . . . TERRY IS SEEN BEHIND THE
BAR SET-UP GLASSES . . . AROUND THE STUDENT PRACTICING SOME STEP
TERRY WALKS IN THE OFFICE . . . GIVES MICHEL A HUG!

TERESSA

My Dear friend, Tomorrow I have to
live to Clearwater. I will come to
see you and help any time you need
me I will always be there for
you . . . Take care my friend . . .

MICHEL (VERY SAD)

C'est la vie . . . It's a big risk I am
taking Terra . . . will try my best.

TERESSA

I know you will make it a success.
you have done it for others . . . you
can do it for yourself . . . bye . . .

SATURDAY NIGHT, IS THE DINER DANCE PARTY . . . CASHIER AT THE DOOR.
ANSWER THE PHONE . . .

JANET (CASHIER)

Millennium Ballroom may I help you?

VERONICA

My name is Veronica, is Michel
available.

JANET

Yes, mam. hold a minute.

MICHEL

Michel Speaking, can I help you?

VERONICA

This is Veronica, You remember me?

MICHEL

Of course Veronica, I am glad you

call. Are you in Florida?

VERONICA
Yes, I am in Davie at my parent, I
show your add in the paper.
congratulations. you have a
student . . .

MICHEL
Great! With your ballet background
We will be performing together. I
can train you as my Professional
partner . . .

VERONICA
This is the goal . . . Can we Start on
Monday at 11:00AM

MICHEL
Absolutely. Good Night. see you on
Monday.

VERONICA
Good night, see you Monday

MONDAY 11:00AM. & MICHEL IS SEEN AT THE BALLROOM REHEARSING THE
COMPAS DANCE . . . THE MAMBO/SALSA DANCE . . .

MICHEL on the Phone!
Daniel,,, Jedam pictures . . . how are
you doing? I need to make a demo DVD
to send to Athens Greece. when can
you come to shoot it.

DANIEL
Let's do it tomorrow. What it's all
about? do you have a script ready to
go . . . ?

MICHEL
Everything is ready, it is about
compas. I also want to shoot the

whole curriculum for the
Merengue/Compas instructional
DVD . . . to teach the kids a new concept of
Dancing the Kompa.

DANIEL (LAUGHING)
You are so crazy, These people will
not care about learning Compas. They
don't care about learning to dance.

DANIEL, MICHEL & VERONICA AT THE EDITING STUDIO, FINISHING THE
DEMO, PLUS MERENGUE COMPAS DANCING AS NEW SOCIAL DANCE ART FORM.
THEY ARE SEATING IN FRONT OF A BIG SCREEN TV WATCHING THE DVD.

Dominique is seen walking in the street, going to her office, they hear noise of car
driving, horns, lot of activities in the street of port-au-prince. An international Call
for her (Juliette from France)

DOMINIQUE (WHISTLE A TRADITIONAL SONG)
DOMINIQUE
Bonjour, bonjour . . . to employees at
her office.

CARLINE (SECRETARY)
Please hold . . . let me get her for you
(over the phone) Madame Dominique
this is a long distance call . . .

DOMINIQUE
Mercie Carline,,, allo, allo. oui
Juliette, how are you doing? how
is the weather in Paris now?

JULIETTE (V. O)
I am doing fine, cannot wait to see
you next week. the weather is
great . . . it is Orleans fest,,, next
month.

DOMINIQUE
I am arriving on Friday july 26,
with air France at Charles de gaules

airport I will keep you posted.

JULIETTE
my sister, send her regards, we
can't wait to see you. We will pick
you up.

DOMINIQUE
Thank you . . . I appreciate that. I
will be in Miami. My friends Michel
and Fong might come to France for
Orleans.

JULIETTE
Your friends are our friends. Dodo,
ma Cherie! I have to let you go . . .
see you next month . . .

DOMINIQUE
see you, next month . . . bye bye.

DOMINIQUE HANG-UP THE PHONE, STARTING TYPING ON THE COMPUTER

on the computer screen
Dear. Michel & Teresa
THIS is TO LET YOU KNOW, I WILL BE
IN PARIS FOR THE ORLEANS FEST., I am
wondering if you will able to make
it this year. will SHOW YOU AROUND
PARIS. I am coming to Miami
tomorrow . . . See you at the Millennium

Gross Bizzzzou

Dominique
DOMINIQUE SINGING HER TRADITIONAL SONG (HAITI CHERIE A CREOLE
POPULAR SONG). DOMINIQUE IS REALLY HAPPY, IS SEEN GOING TO HER
CAR DRIVING HOME.

Michel at his apartment packing up his luggage to his trip . . . plane takes off to
Athens, Greece.

MICHEL IS SEEN IN ATHENS GREECE TEACHING MERENGUE/COMPAS AT THE WORLD DANCE RESEARCH CONGRESS . . . MR RAFTIS PRESENTS THE SHOW. AT THE THEATRE DIFFERENT COUNTRY ARE PERFORMING THEIR TRADITIONAL DANCE ART FORM . . .

In Michel room he is looking at a package: (Surprise). He is asked to perform, at the next Congress in Japan.

his luggage Pack, lives the room.

RANDY (AT HOME DIAL A PHONE NUMBER)
Hey! Michel you are back . . . from your
trip . . . How did it go?

MICHEL
Pretty good . . . how are you.

RANDY
So, you pick me up, today.

MICHEL
Of course . . . I will be there around
4pm . . .

RANDY
Excellent I will be waiting for you.
thank see you my friend at 4pm.

MICHEL & RANDY IN THE CAR GOING TO UNIVERSITY OF MIAMI . . . MICHEL IS DRIVING.

MICHEL
What do you think about Ballroom
dancing as part of education
professor Randy?

RANDY
I think that will be the answer to
keeping the youth off the street . . .

MICHEL
Ballroom Dancing is a Multicultural

study through dance. A good way to
promote diversity. Tell me more
about the Three families of dance.

RANDY (SEATING IN THE PASSANGER SEAT)
Randy explain all . . .

. . .

At the University, Michel and Randy teaching the American Swing. all the Students
line up learning.

AFTER THE LESSON, MICHEL AT THE CAR GOING BACK HOME. THE CELL
PHONE RINGS, JEANNETTE AT THE BALLROOM CALLS.

MICHEL
Jeanette! what going on, I am on my
way.

JEANETTE
You won't believe it, the liquor
board authority came in and cease
your liquor license.

MICHEL
What give them the right to do that
it's a privilege. I don't owe them
any money.

JEANETTE
You are not doing smonky business.
they are waiting for you to sign a
paper . . .

MICHEL
Call Harry Lebon to handle it with
them,,, I will call my lawyer.

JEANETTE
See you when you get here. This is
ridiculous.

AT THE LAWYER OFFICE, MICHEL & HARRY WALK IN. SECRETARY LEAD THEM
TO THE CONFERENCE ROOM . . .

MR. REAGAN
Michel tell me what happen?

MICHEL
The officers from liquor license
office came to the Ballroom Cease
the Liquor license, they live me
this note . . .

MR REAGAN
As of today your operating without
license, Serving of alcoholic
beverage in this establishment is a
violation of the State liquor
law . . . They have no right to come to
your establishment and cease license
of a business in full operation.

Mr. Reagan gets up the chair, Madly, goes to his officer to call the liquor board office
in Margate.

MR REAGAN
Excuse me, My name Reagan the
Attorney for Millennium Ballroom.
who took the liquor license off the
establishment.

SECRETARY
Mr. Mike is the one to talk to, let
me transfer you.

MR MIKE
Mike speaking!

MR REAGAN
Who gave you the right to cease a
license of a business in full
operation, I order you to bring the
license back right now.

MIKE
Who are you, and what license you

are referring to.

MR REAGAN

The Millennium Ballroom, My name
Reagan the attorney for the
business.

MIKE

We were ordered to cease it. you
need to speak to attorney Crazemilo

MR REAGAN

I need the license to be delivered
now . . . My client is in his way to
pick it up.

MR REAGAN TO (MICHEL)

You go to Margate office call me
from there . . . if you don't get it
back.

MICHEL

I am going right now Mr. Reagan.
Harry Lebon, Michel driving on the hwy,,, to Margate office.

HARRY

What they have against us.

MICHEL

I have no idea. What I am going to
do, Without liquor license, I won't be able to pay the rent. The
landlord keep raising the rent every year.

HARRY

There must be someone behind this,
it's absolutely impossible.

MR. REAGAN OVER THE PHONE WITH ATTORNEY CRAZEMILO AT HIS OFFICE.
IN CORAL GABLES.

MR CRAZEMILO (SCHMONK)

Mr. Reagan my client Jack Feldman

dissolves the Corporation and
transfer everything to his name
only. That's why it is possible to
remove the license . . .

MR REAGAN
How are you able to do that, the
State of Florida allowed you to
break the law that govern the united
State of America.

MR CRAZEMILO (SCHMONK)
I have no further answer for you Mr.
Reagan, you govern yourself.

MR REAGAN
Crazemilo enough is enough, I will
see you in court.

MR CRAZEMILO (SCHMONK)
hahaaaaha! laughing . . . hangs up the
phone.

TRANSITION
MICHEL & HARRY AT THE LIQUOR BOARD OFFICE, MIKE, JOHN, LISA
SEATING AT THE CONFERENCE ROOM.

MIKE
Mr. Michel we don't have any thing
against your operation.

JOHN
We have lots of respect for the king
of class you bring to the club
business in our State. people seems
to get envy of you.

LISA
Look! they took you name off the
corporation and transfer the license
to their name, Attorney Crazemilo in
Miami did all the paper work in

Tallahassee.

MIKE
Our office has nothing to do with
that. We can only do what we ordered
to do.

JOHN
Michel, I suggest you to amend the
lease, buy another license and start
over . . .

HARRY
Gentlemen, Thank you for your
help . . . you will hear from us soon.

MICHEL AT THE MANAGEMENT OFFICE MEETING WITH RUDOLPH & TALINA.
HE HAS TO WAIT 1HOUR FOR THEM TO SEE HIM. MICHEL WALK IN THE
OFFICE.

MICHEL
Good morning! I am here to see
Talina, it's an Emergency.

SECRETARY (FRONT DESK)
Please wait; Talina is in a meeting
now. Will leave a message she will
call you back.

MICHEL
I am sorry, I prefer to wait, is Mr.
Rudolph available?

SECRETARY
He cannot help you, you have to
speak to TAlina. follow me and have
a seat here (to the waiting room)

ONE HOUR LATER, RUDOLPH WALK IN. VERY BOSSY
RUDOLPH
Hi! how can we help you.

MICHEL

I am here to see you, and Talina.
What happen to the lease I signed
with you.

RUDOLPH

We have possession of the facility.
Someone turns the key over to us.

TALINA (INVITES MICHEL TO HER OFFICE)

Have a seat, we are in possession of
the facility . . . the lease is being
sold & transferred to Star dance sport
Inc.

MICHEL

What? So, you bleach the contract
with Millennium Ballroom Inc. Some
of my colleague went behind. I know
who.

Talina

From now on don't come to this
office. refer any complaint to our
lawyer . . . Mr. Donald.

MICHEL

Give me him address, I am going to
see him now.

MICHEL AT DANIELLA OFFICE, THE BUSINESS LAWYER.

DANIELLA

Michel, come in . . . have a seat. talk
to me.

MICHEL

I heard someone by the name Jack
Feldman hired Mr. Crazemilo to make
false paper, Change the name of my
corporation and stop us from
operating. we lost the lease, the

sold the liquor license, close the
bank account . . . in Bank of America.

DANIELLA
Absolutely impossible, what is the
landlord phone number . . . in the
midtime let's use your old
Corporation name to get the lease
back on your name only. Amend the
first lease agreement with the
landlord, sign a new lease . . .

MICHEL WENT TO DONALD DUNKIN OFFICE (THE ATTORNEY FOR THE
LANDLORD)

MICHEL
Mr. Dunkin I am here to see how you
can help me solve this . . .

DONALD
This has nothing to do with my
client. It is sad to know what
happen . . . What do you want me to do?

MICHEL
to convince IMA to give the lease
back to me.

DONALD
Money talk! we need two months
security deposit and the first month
rent . . . the lease is now
$12,000/month.

MICHEL
Here is a check for $12.000.00 go
ahead make up a new lease. I was
inspired by the lord to create this
Christian Club, I cannot afford to
let the dream in the hand of evils.

DONALD
I am sorry, I don't take check. Cash
or money order, as I said Money
talk . . . My client wants the full
amount by tomorrow.

MICHEL LIVE THE PARKING LOT—IS SEEN AT A FRIEND OFFICE (MICHELE
ABELLARD . . . WHO'S SORRY, INVEST $100.000.00 IN THE BUSINESS . . . TO
HELP MICHEL WITH HIS DREAM.

ABELLARD
Michel, I heard the ballroom is
closed, We cannot let the mafia win
this time . . . after what happen to
Club Kays.

MICHEL
I won't let it happen, I need at
least 5 more years to prove myself.
I will need someone to buy some
shares and start over.

ABELLARD
How much you need? it's the best
social club to go and get your
stress out. it's also a gold mine.

MICHEL
$350,000 Spent toward opening . . . we
earn a worldwide
reputation . . . Headquarter for
Hallandale section of CID/UNESCO.
with $100.000 You can get 49%
Shares.

ABELLARD
I want to be a silent partner, I
will be there when ever you need
help at the office or at the Bar
during the events.

MICHEL
My lawyer will draw the shareholders
agreement. I will give you 49% of
the business . . . if you decide not to
go on I will ask my Brother to give
you back you investment . . .

ABELLARD
I trust you, and your Brother is my
friend, I spoke to him about the
problem yesterday . . . I have no
problem giving you the money . . . the
whole Community believes in you.

MICHEL
Thank you, Michele . . .(they hug each
other)

ERALY MORNING, GROUP OF FAN STUDENTS READING MIAMI HERALD
NEWSPAPER, THE WHOLE COMMUNITY READING ABOUT THE GRAND
RE-OPENING OF THE NEW CHRISTIAN NIGHT CLUB IN HALLANDALE. THE
NEW MILLENNIUM BALLROOM. WHERE PEOPLE CAN GO TO DANCE TO
HEAL. A NEW SPIRITUAL NIGHT CLUB . . . NO SMOKING, NO ALCOHOL
SERVED . . . THE NEW MILLENNIUM BALLROOM IS BACK IN OPERATION.
STUDENTS SHOWCASE FEATURING: UNIVERSITY OF MIAMI, AND KIDS OF
INTENSITY DANCE STUDIO IN MIAMI LAKE . . .

Michel & Veronica are walking at the beach side . . . making plan to the next trip
to Japan . . . answer the invitation to teach Mambo/Salsa & perform at Erika's
international dance concert in Atsugi, Japan.

MICHEL
Now we need to move on with our
project, the alliance I need to
create w/Asian Choreographers. Erika
& family is the best way to promote
tourism in our town.

VERONICA
I sent her an email to confirm; also
asking to perform Tango, Fox-trot,
Rumba and slow-waltz . . .

MICHEL
Well, we have to teach a workshop on
Mambo/Salsa only.

VERONICA
We will be able to participate every
year, this is the second annual
concert . . . we can bring a demo of our
performance to Erika. when I get to
L. A tomorrow I will Forward another
Email with an attachment of our
Shows.

MICHEL
Great! we might get a second
invitation to perform at the
formation dance piece; poem of the
earth . . . with choreography by Erika &
family . . . Erika's Ballet School . . .

VERONICA
your plane to Japan is from Miami,
Mine from Los-Angeles . . .

MICHEL
I know you are visiting your sister.
we will meet at Tokyo airport. I
will have to wait one hour for your
arrival.

VERONICA
It looks like a movie, we are
making . . .

THE COUPLE EMBRACE, IS GOING TO THE CAR. MICHEL IS SEEN AT
HOME . . . READING MAIL, PAYING BILLS. Veronica IS SEEN IN LOS-ANGELES
IS GETTING IN HER SISTER CAR . . . THEN IN A RESTAURENT EATING, GREAT
CONVERSATION IN CHINESE LANGUAGE.

HILDEGADE (VERONICA'S SISTER)
So, you are going to Tokyo . . . to
teach with Michel.

VERONICA
I didn't want to go, It's very
important to Michel to have
affiliation with Japan.

HIDEGADE
For you it's a way to visit your
part of our country. you have not
been there for years.

VERONICA
Ballroom Dancing is growing fast in
Japan & china now . . . we may be able
to travel more often . . . in the
future.

TOKYO AIRPORT (INSIDE THE AIRPORT MICHEL GREETING HIS NEW
COLLEAGUE: KAN-ICHI. VERONICA IS IN HER SISTER'S CAR DRIVING TO
LOS-ANGELES AIRPORT. US AIRWAY LANDING IN TOKYO . . .

Michel, Veronica and KAN-ICHI are in a bus going to Atsugi from Tokyo airport.
crossing the flying bridge, view of the port . . . Erika (who's organizing the international
concert) is walking to her Ballet school in Atsugi early morning.

INT: (CLASSROOM) MICHEL IS TEACHING A WORKSHOP IN MAMBO/SALSA.
LOTS JAPONNESE KIDS TAKING THE CLASS.

Michel
Let's have, let's have everybody
line behind me.

KAN-ICHI . . .
. . .
(Translates in Japanese
language))

MICHEL
Ballroom dancing was the first mean
of communication created for
married couple. Before we do the
Mambo/Salsa, let's do a little
exercise together, using a Cha cha

music.

Michel is teaching (chachacha slide) Kids learning in class. Chacha music playing (Kids Students dancing Chacha slide) together with Michel and Veronica . . . Press people in the background . . . curiously taking pictures.

MICHEL (V. O)
Now we are ready to Mambo/Salsa.
Salsa is a new generation name for mambo . . . the
characteristic of the Salsa dance is
a pause, dancers need to do on the
4&1 beats of the music, a breaking
action will occur on the second
beat; let's start with basic . . .

Three basic figures are being taught to the students . . . the
all get it well enough to start dancing it as couple.

MICHEL
learning to dance is similar to the
way we learn how to write. At first
we makes letters after we put them
together to make phrases etc. in
dancing we learn steps, we put
together to communicate with each
other on the dance floor.

EVERY BODY IS SEEN COMBINE THE THREE FIGURES TOGETHER WHILE DANCING . . .

At the Hotel; Michel & Veronica enjoying their stay in Tokyo. at the bar having a glass of wine . . . listening to traditional music of Japan . . . are seen going to the hotel room.

MICHEL (ON THE ROOM COMPUTER)
Ok. now, time to see what happening
at the New millennium in Florida.

VERONICA
Yes, yes you can send an email to
Randy to have a look at those crooks
stealing your profits . . .

MICHEL
Yap, you are right, new millennium
ballroom is a public domain. we are
working just to put money at the
landlord pocket . . .

Veronica is in the bathroom getting ready taking a shower, then (in bathtub). Michel
sitting at the desk writing some notes . . .

MICHEL (V. O WHILE WRITING)
It is not when we study the ordinary
pursuit of man that history becomes
interesting. One of the brightest threads in the
fabric of man, s evolution has been
his love of dancing. dance has
marked birth, marriages, and death.
Celebration for planting, harvesting
also called for dance. dancing
chased away evil spirits and cure
the sick. Ballroom dancing was
probably the first form of dance
that was purely designed for their
own amusement. 1776 was the most
important year in the history of
ballroom dancing when the most
spirited and divine dance (the
waltz) appeared in Vienna. This was
the first real couple dance when
they actually touched and had closed
contact.
Few couples is seen on a grand salon dancing a beautiful
Vienna waltz. Music & V. O in the Background (mix Video
layers)

Michel (V. O) continues
It became the way that boy met girl
and the way that the working class
enjoyed his money in the company of
his lady. it is for all ages, all
sizes, all classes, creeds an
colors.

MICHEL
We got an email from Dominique.
Dominique will be in Paris. We
should take advantage of a good
vacation.

VERONICA (COMING OUT OF THE BATHROOM.)
That will be great . . . Imagine us in
Paris we do not know where to go.
Without Dominique; you would go by
yourself. for all that happening in
the Ballroom you need a vacation.

MICHEL
let's go! my first time to Orleans'
festival. One of the France
traditional event of the year.

MICHEL IS SEEN IN TOKYO TOURIST AREA WITH VERONICA,,, AND FRIENDS
FAMILY, EATING LUNCH TRADITIONAL JAPONNESE COOKING, GOING TO
THE TEMPLE OF BOODHA . . . PUBLIC & TOURISTS PLACE LOT OF PEOPLE.

TRANSITION

MICHEL AT TOKYO AIRPORT, STUDENTS WAVING GOODBYE, HAVE A NICE
TRIP PROF. YAMAMOTO (V. O) PLANE LANDING AT CHARLES THE GALLES
AIRPORT.

TRANSITION

A beautiful view of Eiffel-tower. Paris birds, building, monuments. Michel & Veronica
check in at the Hotel in Paris . . . in the room . . . Michel is seen watching TV-French
Program, Veronica at the window over-looking at the street view . . . lots of traffic . . .
beautiful trees . . .

MICHEL
It's been 25 years I haven't spoken
a word in French. Two weeks in Paris
I will remember all my French

VERONICA
You speak better than I do. you

understand Dominique very well . . .

MICHEL
Dominique is my French tutor. I
learn a lot from her . . .

DOMINIQUE IS SEEN AT CLUB BELLEVUE IN PORT-AU-PRINCE GETTING
READY FOR THE FASION SHOW . . . A FEW SHOTS FROM THE FASHION
SHOW . . . THE ARTIST, LAROSILIER, DOMINIQUE ARE SEEN IN THE EXIBIT.
LOVE MUSIC PLAYING . . . HAPPY . . . SCENE.

FADE TO DOMINIQUE AT HOME PACKING SUITCASE TO PARIS . . .

TRANSITION

PLANE LANDING IN PARIS . . . MICHEL AND Veronica IN THE HOTEL ROOM,
GOING TO BATHROOM . . . MICHEL READY FOR BED, IS SEEN SEATING AT
THE DESK WRITING . . . BEAUTIFUL MUSIC KEELING ME SOFTLY.

Early morning Dominique is walking on the walkway, crossing the street busy traffic.
At the hotel . . . meeting Veronica & Michel. The three friends sitting in a family
restaurant.

A view of the Eifel Tower is seen, lot of activities, bird flying . . . Dominique is seeing
with Veronica walking together in champ Elyse, in front of the tower.

DOMINIQUE
Tell me How was your trip to Japan?

VERONICA
We have been invited again next year
to perform at the 3rd annual
international Concert, That's a
great privilege. a great way to
promote ballroom dancing in Asia.

DOMINIQUE
You know, Michel deserve lots of
credits, the man works his buts off
spending all his accumulated
knowledge and life time savings to
build new millennium ballroom

. Michel told
me: The landlord raises the rent to
$13,000.00/month plus $11,000, this
year on property tax . . . they are
forcing him to give all up.

VERONICA

Yes . . . It is a dream Salon,
The ballroom program he creates help
bring people all over the world to
the shopping center. Hallandale Bch
become, the capital city of the
world.

DOMINIQUE

You're absolutely right. When he
started Club Kay's Starlight
Ballroom, the first multicultural
club in south Florida. Before, you
could see no cars driving in the
town, the old diplomat mall was a
rat's house, nothing happening, it
was all dead.

VERONICA

Yap! Community service, No reward
Michel took it from his dad. The
city official did nothing to support
his Ballroom studio.

DOMINIQUE

Oh lala! His dad is a legend for
what he did for people. it's
incredible . . .

VERONICA

I went a few time to visit. the
family value is in good education
more than making money . . . they carry
their bank account in the wrong
place: (their head . . .) Who cares
about good education today, if you

don't have money in the bank.

DOMINIQUE (LAUGHING)
Yah,,, yap, Who cares about that,
money is power now, beautiful poems
doesn't put food on the table . . . the
world setting is out of hand.

VERONICA (LAUGHS)
It is very . . . very Scary world to
live today. The economy is going no
where . . . no one is making money in
the stock market . . .

Dominique is seen Bravely Laying down on top of a high old Government building
outside wall . . . Having a sun tan . . . Happy to be in Paris.

DOMINIQUE (V. O)
Michel is trying to make the compas
part of Ballroom dancing,,, who's
going to learn it. the people in the
Island do not care about national
Identity & social values . . . Now it's
hip-pop, rave and bachata all
over . . .

VERONICA
Hip-hop is the kind of sound of noise.
created as a destruction to the
youth. it leads them to drugs, sex
and alcohol

DOMINIQUE
You dam right! As, you guy trying
to teach to the world. Dancing to
the wrong timing to music, creates a
disorientation of the brain
settings . . . Dancers with this kind of
listening problem will develop lack
of discipline in their life.

VERONICA (LAUGHING)
That is exactly what happen, Lack of
discipline, the World is disorganize
by people like the landlords who,
never learn to dance properly they
grew up with ways to steal other
people own creative works. They
have money, They make their own
rules.

Veronica & Dominique are seen at the Train station waiting. Then in Orleans, picking
up friends to new Orleans Fest. At the friend's house . . . (greeting . . . Juliette &
Jeannine happy to see everybody)

JULIETTE
Let's go, let's go . . . My boy friend
is waiting for me at the fest. We
are late.

JEANNINE (OTHER THE SISTER)
Tell me Dominique, what about the
School now. Can we do something in
Port-prince . . . opening a business
and vocational tutoring for the
French speaking youth to get some
sort of professional degree.

DOMINIQUE
That a great idea . . . the country is
in need of everything . . . the Diaspora
is working hard to help
rebuilding . . . there is hope . . .

JULIETTE
Let's do it . . .

JEANINE (SHOWING PAPPER WORK)
Here, here! this is all the subjects
the system used now at the
University in Paris, we wrote and
develop the whole tutorial system
for The Board of education here . . .

JULIETTE
Yes . . . Dominique You can use it for
your school . . . Beside they people
speak French.

The phone rings Juliette runs, great conversation in the
background a good friend of Dominique (a Diaspora in France)

JULIETTE
Hallo Gerald . . . good . . . at what time?
we all going to be there. your
friend Dominique with 2 other guests
are coming also.

JULIETTE
Dominique it's Gerald our friend
best friend . . .

DOMINIQUE (VERY EXCITED)
My god Gerald! Give me the phone,
let' me speak to him. (Grab the
phone from Juliette)

DOMINIQUE
Mon amour, Gerald comment vas-tu?

GERALD (V. O)
Dominique! Ma Cherie, Lord! it's
five years since I left the
country . . . I am coming to join you
all later . . .

DOMINIQUE
We are on our way to Orleans fest.
you have to be part of the summit
this year, for the development of
tourism. by Wilfrid Belfort the
organizer.

GERALD (V. O)
This country will not go anywhere.
Nothing will work (the people!)

Dominique relocate (bedroom) Special music is heard the
phone dip conversation. Educational system . . . juliette, veronica,
Jeanine is seen in the living room . . .

JULIETTE
So, Veronica are you Chinese or
Japanese?

VERONICA
Both. half & half.

JEANINE
What do you mean Both? (curiously)

JULIETTE
So, you speak 3 languages.

VERONICA
Actually!!! more than 3 . . .

JEANINE
Oh! I know, you dance ballroom! that
is right . . . Ballroom Dance is a
multicultural Language.

VERONICA
Yes, we Dance Ballroom and produce
Ballroom dance instructional DVD'S
Michel makes the compas social
dance, to promote a new way in the
concept of social dancing. for kids.
If everybody do ballroom there
won't be any barrier in spoken languages.

JULIETTE
That is right! Spoken language is
confusing sometime . . . We have a copy
of your DVD . . . I want to buy the
whole collection. you and Michel are
fantastic teachers.

JEANINE
Magnum band Plays the best Compas
Music . . . The real Kompa Music . . . they
play a lot on the radio here in
France.

JULIETTE
Oh yaa! in French we say
Compas (C. O. M. P. A. S) to describe the
Dance Art Form (the Movement &
gestures) and K. O. M. P. A to the Music
art form.

TRANSITION

EVERY BODY IS LIVING, IS SEEN IN A CAR DRIVING AWAY . . . CONVERSATION
CONTINUE . . . DOMINIQUE, JEANINE, MICHEL, Veronica & JULIETTE EASY
TRAFIC . . . CONSTRUCTION ARE SEEN IN THE BACKGROUND. FESTIVAL
ACTIVITY IN ORLEANS, FRENCH ARTIST COMEDIAN MOVIE STAR MR.
JACQUES DUMOND . . . A FRIEND OF DOMINIQUE IS DOING SOME ACTING . . .
AND DOMINIQUE, JEANINE THE WHOLE CREW ARRIVE TO ORLEANS FEST.
LOT OF ACTIVITIES . . .

DOMINIQUE
Regardez-moi Monsieur et Dame . . . Le
grand . . . grand historian Jacques
Dumont . . . (translates with titles)

DOMINIQUE
Voila des journeaux, publications de
tous ses oeuvres du passee.

DOMINIQUE SHOWING PICTURES OF JACQUES DUMOND FROM A
NEWSPAPPER PUBLICATION. JACQUES A VERY FAMOUS COMEDIAN AND
HISTORIAN IN FRANCE . . . A VIEW OF THE WHOLE FESTIVITIES IS SEEN AND
FADE OUT TO. DOMINIQUE & FONG IN THE TRAIN GOING BACK TO PARIS
FROM ORLEANS CITY.

DOMINIQUE
So, Veronica I t will be great to do a
presentation of your future plan at
the summit.

VERONICA
Wilfrid proposed us to be part. it
is not a bad idea.

MICHEL
We will also do a performance . . . For
them in Miami . . .

VERONICA
we are living to Florida
tomorrow . . . we will send a letter of
invitation to Mr. Raftis who will
present his agenda About CID/UNESCO

DOMINIQUE
Ouaw . . . CID is the umbrella
organization within UNESCO for all
form of dance in the world . . . If he
can come, Wilfrid will be happy . . .

MICHEL
He is not paying for that. It's a
sacrifice . . . we have to make to
create a better image . . .

VERONICA
Michel wants his presentation, to
be Followed by Mr. Raftis Speech on
the value of dance.

THE WHOLE CROWD IS SEEN! LOT OF FESTIVITIES . . . HISTORIES.

TRANSITION

MICHEL, VERONICA AND DOMINIQUE AT THE SUMMIT, LOTS OF ACTIVITIES.
MR RAFTIS THE PRESIDENT OF THE INTERNATIONAL DANCE COUNCIL, IN
MIAMI IS PRESENTING THE VALUE OF DANCE, TO THE AUTHORITIES . . .
CARL FOMBRUM A JOURNALIST INTRODUCED MICHEL ON STAGE . . .
MICHEL IS PRESENTING THE FOUNDATION OF THE INTERNATIONAL
DANCE COUNCIL, SECTION OF HALLANDALE, HOLLYWOOD FLORIDA. ITS
ACTIVITIES, AND IMPORTANCE OF BALLROOM DANCING IN THE SCHOOL

SYSTEM . . .$10 MILLION DOLLARS A YEAR WILL BE RAISED TO HELP FINANCE
GOVERNMENT PROJECT.

MR. RAFTIS
Good Evening Ladies & Gentlemen!
C. I. D is a friend term for:
Conseil International de la Dance
Meaning: International dance
Council . . . This Organization was form
within the Unesco office in Paris,
as you know, there is an
Organization for every science,
every arts and every Culture within
Unesco. C. I. D is the Umbrella
Organization for all form of Dance
in the world . . .

TRANSITION

MICHEL
Power point presentation is shown on
big screen TV.

TRANSITION

THE LANDLORD MR. CARLOS & MIGUEL AT ROCK & ASSOCIATES, TALKING
ABOUT THE DANCE STUDIO. ANOTHER CONFRONTATION . . .

MR CARLOS
Miguel, I went to the Ballroom in
our center in Hallandale bch. blvd.
This place has lots of potentials . . . it's perfect for
Restaurant night Club.

HENRY
With the economy the way it is now.
we can have our own people run it as
a high class restaurant night club
and make a lot of money.

MIGUEL
Michel is a hard working man, he's

been there for 8 years, he has no
intention to give it up.

MR CARLOS

I know he want to renew the lease
for another term . . . it's not going to
happen. you have to make up some
excuses . . .

HENRY

He is behind the rent, use that
excuse.

MIGUEL

Employee works according to the
boss. you remember giving him delays
to come up with the money . . . what
about the new lease you have me
wrote to him.

CARLOS

It is not signed by any body.

MIGUEL

This is a well educated teacher in
the field. He is looking to bring
investors/shareholders to change it
for the better . . . I believe we, will
have a good tenant.

HENRY

Bullshit! his business plan he is
trying to sell won't work . . . he will
not have a lease. I need the
facility . . . I can make more money . . .

CARLOS

I don't give a dam . . . Money
talk . . . Ron have the maintenance
clean up the place . . . someone is
taking it over in October.

MIGUEL

You, are giving Sam the key? to run
the same operations . . . He is been a
good tenant for 8 years . . . he's only
behind for one month.

CARLOS

Henry, Have the lock change right
now, this is my order . . . I do not
want him there any more, We need
money . . . I just take over the center.
We cannot afford tenant behind the
rent . . .

MICHEL IS GOING TO THE STUDIO TO TEACH A COUPLE. HE PARKS HIS
CAR. THE COUPLE TAMMY AND ANDY ARE WAITING OUTSIDE THE DOOR.
MICHEL TRY TO OPEN. THE KEY CAN NOT OPEN THE DOOR . . . MAKES A
PHONE CALL TO THE LANDLORD . . .

MICHEL

Let me speak to Arnold or Don
Please.

MIGUEL (V. O)

Allo! this is Arnold, What can I do
for you . . .

MICHEL

You Change the lock, I cannot get
in my studio . . .

MIGUEL

Hold on, let me put Henry on the
phone with you.

HENRY (THREE WAY CALL)

You have to bring me money now, or
you are out. we are putting it out
for lease . . .

MICHEL

What right do you have to close my

business in full operation without
an eviction letter . . .

MIGUEL
We are losing money, Michel, people
wants to lease the place . . . money
talk.

MICHEL
Didn't you gave me the Month of
august free to renew the lease to
start in November. What is going on
Now?

HENRY
The maintenance, will come to open
the door, I have them clean up
everything. I put it up for
lease . . . if you have any thing that
is not attach to the fixtures you
have one hour to move them out.

MICHEL HANG UP THE PHONE,,,, THE COUPLE STUDENT GOING TO THE
PARKING LOT WITH HIM.

TAMMY
I cannot believe you, just . . . said
nothing, they cannot close your
business after 8 years . . . just like
that.

Andy
you should see your lawyer about
this. beside what happen to all your
personal properties.

MICHEL
My best lawyer is the lord. He was
the one who gave me the courage to
build this place . . . with his guidance
I survived 8 years, I will find a
way.

TAMMY
Ok. Michel let us know, where we can
continue our lessons. It is not fair
what happen to you.

MICHEL
I may have to change my career to
digital film making . . . I will let you
know . . . have a nice day.

TRANSITION

SAMIEL AT THE LANDLORD OFFICE NEGOCIATES THE LEASE

MIGUEL
Sam! come in . . .(a
the office) have a
seat.

SAMIEL
What I want is the lease sign to my
name, once I have that I can
convince investors to buy the whole
gad dam business . . . the Business plan
is a good one, people will be
interested.

MIGUEL
We need to find a way to take his
liquor license with the place.

SAMIEL
Absolutely, Wait . . . I have an idea. I
am going to give an offer he can't refuse.

MIGUEL
whatever, here is a lease agreement,
sell the whole thing. I gave you 3
weeks . . . to find me a tenant with
Money . . .

SAMIEL

You got it! take care, I will see
what I can do. What about his
Deposit and all his personal
properties . . .?

MIGUEL

Everything under control, pretend to
be his partner . . . until you transfer
the all license to your name.

SAMIEL SHAKES HIS HAND AND LEAVES . . . IN HIS CAR GOING HOME. HIS
SON CALL . . . TO FIND OUT ABOUT THE BALLROOM . . .

SAMSON

Dad did you get it?

SAMIEL

Of course, I am not giving either
one a penny . . . And I will get the
Liquor license also . . .

SAMSON

If you can do that, it will be
great . . . laughing . . . I will own a
ballroom with no money down. OK dad
see you when you get home.

SAMIEL

Samson! let me call Michel and give
him a key to the place . . . we need all
his contacts . . . after all the
electricity bills is still on his
name . . . he is paying for it.

SAMSON

remember Rock does not want him
around . . .

SAMIEL

I will take care of that too . . . see
you later . . .

SAMSON

Nothing to lose Dad . . . go for it. If
we can get the business phone Back
on, that will bring us the whole
customer base.

SAMIEL

That's a good idea, Son go online
register with the State: Copa
Tropical Inc. you are the
President . . . it only cost $87.

SAMSON

I love Florida . . . Dad I will meet you
at the Ballroom . . . we need to talk on
the Management.

SAMIEL

See you . . . at the house . . . You you do
not have to meet me there. bye.
bye.

TRANSITION

MICHEL IS SEEN IN HIS SUV-TRUCK PARKING LOT AT UNIVERSITY OF MIAMI.
WALKING TO THE CLASSROOM— . . . ALEX IN A MEETING WITH ALL THE
STUDENTS. ASKING MICHEL WHAT DANCE TO TEACH FOR THE NEW SEASON.
STUDENTS READY FOR DANCE LESSON.

ALEX

Michel! I want you to end the class
on time today, you give way too
much . . . remember they are all novice
dancers.

MICHEL

I know what they need.
ALEX (MAKE A FACE)
8pm . . . ok.

MICHEL

You got it boss . . .

MICHEL (ADRESSING TO THE CLASS)
let's have everybody with high
heels behind me . . . those who have
never wear heels in front of me.
Michel (Close up, Silence (music sound effect, Suspense, all
students are curiously listening . . .

MICHEL
lack of communication leads to lack
of discipline, mistrust and respect,
divorce . . . you mane it. we need to
learn dancing as a way to
communicate ourselves with others. A
new concept in dance that needed to
be taught so, long neglected . . . The
priority have been given to written
and verbal communication . . . there are
school all over the world where one
can go to learn medicine,
architecture, to become a lawyer, an
accountant etc.
There are none for choreographers.
etiquettes of body language . . . the
notations of our body line in
choreology . . . that's what
missing . . . in the schooling
system . . .

PROF. RANDY
Enough B. S . . . come on Michel let's
go . . .(very mad)

MICHEL (IGNORING RANDY)
we are going to work on our posture
the body we use to go to the shap
shop is not! not the same as what
we use on the dance floor . . .

VERONICA (ASSISTANT TEACHER, CLOSE UP)
Yes! posture is our genetic and
cultural heritage . . .

MICHEL
No one has the same posture, there
are as many type of posture as there
are people in the world

STUDENTS
Is it what they call styles . . .
RANDY
Exactly! Let's do a little exercise
together with music . . .

Randy, Michel, Veronica and all the students joining in the dance exercise with
music . . .

SAMIEL AT THE CLUB OFFICE MAKING A PHONE CALL,,, PHONE RING THREE
TIMES (V. O) THANK YOU FOR CALLING THE NEW MILLENNIUM BALLROOM
I CAN NOT COME TO THE PHONE, PLEASE LEAVE YOUR NAME NUMBER
AND MESSAGE, I WILL GET BACK TO YOU AS SOON AS I CAN. REMENBER
YOUR CALLS ARE VERY IMPORTANT TO US . . . WE WILL GET BACK TO YOU
AS SOON AS WE SWING TO THE DOOR.

SAMIEL (V. O) CLASS IS GOING ON
HaHaHalo, Michel, I think we have a
deal . . . I have the key for the place,
we can work together. Let's meet
tonight . . . I will be waiting at the
ballroom . . . Hang up . . .

MICHEL (IN CLASS UM.)
Understanding of our own posture,
and able to use it fluently to
music . . . May lead society to peace.
Let's get a partner . . .

All couple dancing American Style Swing . . . Class is over . . .
Students happy about the lessons . . . outside going home . . .
MICHEL IS SEEN AT A RESTAURENT WITH SAMIEL . . .

SAMIEL
I told you I have interest in the
Ballroom. It a great location, we
can work together . . .

MICHEL

How can we work together? the rent
is too high . . .

SAMIEL

I do have my way to negotiate with
Ma . . . mmmafia such as Rock &
Associate people . . . They are evil . . .

MICHEL

This is, the whole Business plan.
review it. I have been planning &
working on this for 8
years . . . nothing else will make
cnough to pay this high rent.

SAMIEL

I do not want Ballroom. you can run
your Dance program . . . I will take
care of high Class diner Dance and
show . . . which I already know what to
do.

MICHEL

Samuel, Papa Sammy as I used to call
you . . .

SAMIEL (CUT IN)

ya ya ya! you remember me, next door
to Club Kays . . . you used to bring
thousand people to Party there on
week end

MICHEL

Those time is way passed, now is the
Russian Club/Restaurant . . .

Samuel

We need to make a deal on your
liquor License . . . I will pay all the
business bills . . . you do not have to
wooowory . . . about Rock people.

MICHEL
Right now, everything sounds
good . . . you need to come up with
$10.000.00 to keep me going for a
few month . . . I am so depressed, I am
not able to work the same way again
for a while . . .

SAMIEL
Let's go to call your lawyer to make
a contract of transfer.

MICHEL
I will pick you up tomorrow morning
and discuss it more . . . if you come up
with $10.000. We will be partners.

SAMIEL
Thank you Michel, see you tomorrow
Morning. you can pick me up at home.
Goodnight . . .

MICHEL
Good night, Sammy.

A VIEW OF HALLANDALE BCH BLVD BRIDGE IS GOING UP, OVER LOOKING
THE INTERCOASTAL . . . BEAUTIFUL SKY, WATER, BIG BUILDING & THE
SUNSET . . . TRANSITION

SAMIEL AND MICHEL IS IN THE CAR, DRIVING TO HALLANDALE FROM THE
MEETING IN NORTH MIAMI . . . MICHEL IN THE CAR MAKES A CALL . . .

MICHEL (ON HIS CELL PHONE DRIVING)
Mr. Borno please, this is Michel
Jacques from New Millennium
ballroom.

MR BORNO (OVER THE PHONE)
Michel how can I help you?

MICHEL
Mr. Borno, I am here with Mr. Samuel

the new leasee & buyer. As you know,
I am not in operation any more. I
want to transfer the contract to
Copa tropical Inc.

MR. BORNO
It's not a problem, it will only
cost $250.00 in paper work. what's
the deal.

MICHEL
Copa tropical Inc, will buy the
License for $135.000. Assume the
mortgage payment of $1,374.00/month.
with $10.000 down to New millennium
Ballroom . . . plus $2000.00/month
toward paying the balance off.

MR BORNO
That's all right to me. I will fax
the contract to your Number . . . for
both parties to sigh, Notarize and
fax it back to me . . .

MICHEL & SAMIEL
Have a nice day . . . Mr. borno. Thank you.

SAMIEL, MICHEL & SAMSON AT THE BALLROOM OFFICE MAKING PLAN . . .
MICHEL'S DAILY PROGRAM IS SCHEDULED TO START ON

OCTOBER 1, 2008 . . .
SAMIEL
Ok, Samson! the arrangement with new
Millennium is this: Michel will run
the dance program as he always
do . . . We will bring the night
business as we discussed.

SAMSON
I know! I know. we have nothing to
do with Ballroom dancing, it's
Michel baby . . .

MICHEL

For me to come in here and work my
daily programming, I would need 50%
of what come to the door. 100% bar
business we should be able to do
good.

SAMSON

You pay your staff and marketing . . .

MICHEL

yes, Advertising, and Staff on me.
Do not worry . . . You can seat back
collect all the money and pay the
bills on time.

SAMIEL

It's alright, that case you have no
woorry. you see, Samson I told you
Michel would work something out with
us.

MICHEL

Ok! give me the key . . . I will bring
everybody back to work . . . Make a
contract . . . I will have my lawyer
reformat it . . . Any way we are in
business. I have to go. good
night . . .

TRANSITION

MICHEL & VERONICA MEET AT THE DIPLOMAT HOTEL, OVER LOOKING
THE SEA . . .

VERONICA

So, what happen in your meeting with
those guys.

MICHEL

Well this is the deal! $10.000 down
on the liquor license plus

$2000/month. 50% from the door
income of all the dance program up
to 10pm. They will create a classy
dinner dance & Vegas type of shows
with full liquor Bar, hopefully they
will make enough to survive all
bills.

VERONICA
Bull shit Absolutely impossible.
Who's paying for the loan on the
liquor license.

MICHEL
They will also . . . wait a minute, it's
a lot of money when sum up . . .

VERONICA
You see, this is another crooked
business negotiations . . . these guys
walk in a well established business,
they have no idea how to make it
work . . . with no money . . . Do the
math . . .

MICHEL
Rent $15,000.00 + liquor license
Payment $ 1400.00 + $2,000.00 to you
+ $1,200.00 light bill +++++

VERONICA
You out of mind my dear . . . I am out
of this B. S. No way they will pay
you . . . You transfer the license, they
will kick you out . . . you may not see
a penny . . . wait to see. if they will
come with a contract . . .

MICHEL
You are absolutely right . . . people
with money will not act like they
do. I have nothing to worry,

Consider this a year vacation to
learn . . . Digital film making . . . I will
have a lot of True story to tell . . .

VERONICA
you sure do . . . With all those bad
experience . . . you are a pioneer in
dealing with bad people.

MICHEL
Oh boy! let's Change the subject . . .

FADE IN TO DEBBIE AT THE COUNTER DESK (NEW LOCATION: CLUB
TROPICAL) GUY LEMONIER A SOUND ENGINEER . . . AT THE COUNTER . . .
DEBBIE ENTERS)

GUY
Hi!!! babe . . . How are you? you save
me a dance tonight.

DEBBIE (HUGGING)
of course babe . . . Michel invited me
to come and sing a few songs at the
Party tonight . . . but, do you think
they will be people . . . he closed
millennium. this is the first time
at this Club . . .

GUY
You kidding there will be people.
they all will love your singing . . . I
am happy myself you are here . . .

BEBBIE
I will see you later.

GUY
See ya! baby, don't forget save me a
dance . . .

BEBBIE IS LIVING THE PARKING LOT, VERY SEXY . . . GUY IS HAPPY HE HAVE
TO DANCE COMPAS W/AN AMERICAN STAR SINGER TO SHOW OFF . . . HE

IS SETTING UP THE PA SOUND SYSTEM FOR MAGNUM BAND . . . THE BAND
REHEARSING . . . PEOPLE START COMING IN SLOWLY . . . TO A FULL HOUSE . . .
MAGNUM BAND MUSIC . . . OH LA, LA. PLAYING . . .

TRANSITION

DEBBIE, GUY WALK TO THE BAR,,, SITTING TOGETHER IN A DIALOG. DIMITRY
ANOTHER DANCE TEACHER WALK TO THE DOOR, HAPPY TO SEE DEBBIE . . .
JOIN THE CONVERSATION.

At the university of Miami, Students living to cars going home . . . couple guys and
girl talking . . . into becoming a dance teacher, if they take it more serious . . . going
to their car. a few cars starts moving, cut to Michel, driving with Randy talking about
three families of dance . . . live on the highway 1-95 going to club tropical. People
dancing Compas in very dark room.

> DEBBIE
> Ho my god, How they can dance in the
> dark? it looks very vulgar the way
> they move, look at this couple oh
> lord . . . Dimitry! this's not the way
> to dance. It's a Shame.

> GUY
> That the way the people dance in
> Club . . . it is part of their culture.

> DIMITRY
> No guy, Mon cher . . . talk for yourself
> and these people . . .
> (laughing . . . laughing everybody are
> laughing . . . Debbie, guy,
> dimitry . . . two other couple at the
> bar . . .)

> DEBBIE
> This is pure sex on the floor. the
> Music is so beautiful . . . I could make
> the most graceful movements to this
> music look . . .(bebbie dancing by
> herself . . .

GUY

I am telling you, bebe (flirting
with Debbie pulling her hand) let's
go dancing?

DEBBIE

NO, no no . . . not with me find
yourself a prostitute . . . I am not
staying too long . . . I will sing and
live . . . I am afraid to dance with
stranger like that . . .

GUY

I am not stranger baby!

BEBBIE

I mean girl-friends, Boy-friends,
It's not too bad to dance like that
with your wife/husband,,, but! it too
dark, no one can see each
other . . . what the reason to
dance . . . you can stay home and make
love . . .

THE BAND STOP PLAYING, THE MASTER OF CEREMONY ANNOUNCES
DEBBIE ON STAGE . . . ALL LIGHT TURN ON. MICHEL, RANDY, VERONICA A
FEW STUDENTS AND GUESTS ARE SEEN WALKING IN THE DOOR . . . DEBBIE
ON STAGE . . . SINGING . . . (DIMITRY W/PARTNER, RODRIGUE W/PARTNER
DANCING ON THE FLOOR BEAUTIFULL FOX-TROT . . . RANDY W/PARTNER,
ALL THE STUDENTS, MICHEL AND VERONICA JOIN ON THE DANCE FLOOR.
PEOPLE APLAUDING TO EACH SONG . . . MAGNUM BAND TAKE OVER
THE STAGE . . . SAME COUPLES ARE ON THE DANCE FLOOR DANCING
BEAUTIFULLY TO COMPAS MUSIC . . .

BEBBIE

Ok! guy let's dance now, it's more
acceptable, we can see each other.

GUY

I can do Ballroom Compas . . . let's go,
I will show you.

Bebbie let's see who can teach who
how to dance . . .

(couple walk to the floor and start dancing)

TRANSITION

MICHEL AT HOME OPENING THE FRONT DOOR. IS SEEN IN THE LIVING
ROOM TAKING A GLASS OF WINE . . . MICHEL IN THE BEDROOM UN-DRESS
FROM THE PARTY, AT THE SHOWER . . . LEAVING SHOWER, AT THE BED,
WATCHING T. V . . . HIS COMPAS INSTRUCTIONAL DANCE DVD IS PLAYING . . .
MICHEL IS IN DEEP THINKING . . . NO, NO, NO HE PICKS UP THE PHONE
DIAL A #

TRANSITION

VERONICA AT HER HOUSE EATING ICE CREAM BEFORE GOING TO BED.
LISTENING TO MUSIC BEETHOVEN . . . VERONICA GET UP TO GO TO THE
BEDROOM THE PHONE RINGS. (MICHEL V. O IN BACKGROUND) VERONICA
IS WALKING TO THE BEDROOM . . .

MICHEL
Sorry to call so late . . . Samuel want
to meet with me tomorrow at 11am . . .

VERONICA
Again, something is wrong w/those
people . . .

MICHEL
I have the impression that for real
He might be a good human being to
work with.

VERONICA
I am so tired now, You should make a
movie out of all this . . . the $10.000
investment will prove him
right . . . Bare with me, you won't see
a dime from this man . . .

MICHEL
You always right, I will see you
tomorrow. good night . . .

VERONICA
Good night . . .

EXT- EARLY MORNING, SAMIEL AND HIS WIFE, UNLOCK THE STUDIO
DOOR . . . WALK TO THE OFFICE . . .

SAMIEL (TO HIS WIFE)
we have to make up a note for him to
sign. Then the transfer of the
license will be easy . . .

WIFE
Hue, hue . . . Steven is coming to type
it . . . before he gets here . . . you have
to think, write it down.

SAMIEL
I am going to pee . . . this fucken
prostate . . . killing me . . .(is seen
walking to the men room bad leg)

MICHEL MEETS WITH SAMSON IN THE PACKING LOT, THEY SHAKE HAND
LIKE PARTNERS. ARE SEEN WALK IN THE OFFICE . . . SAMIEL, WIFE . . . MICHEL
IS STANDING,,, REFUSES TO SIT DOWN . . .

SAMIEL
Have a seat Michel . . . We need to
discuss serious business . . . we want
you to make a good living here . . .

SAMSON
Yes . . . you know everything about the
business . . . you build the whole
place. Our plan will work . . .

MICHEL
well let's get to the point.
Everything I own is right here. You

need no furniture thing to buy . . . the
customers are ready . . . just
licensing . . .

SAMIEL
This, also Samson we need to go to
the city hall and apply . . .

MICHEL
I have been running a gentleman
business for 8 years in the
city . . . September 31th, my license is
not yet renewed . . . how are you going
to start operation tomorrow?

SAMSON
Millennium liquor license is good
active to March 31, 2008. for the
bar we are legal . . .

SAMIEL
Tha, da, that's what count the most
for me . . . the bar business . . .

MICHEL
I will renew my city license, you
have the contract I gave you from
Mr. Borno, sign it, I will have it
notarized . . . with The $10.000 check
deposit . . . I will prove what I can do
for you . . .

SAMIEL
Something need to be changed in the
contract . . .

MICHEL
I have to go . . . let me know what
happen. in the midtime . . . I am doing
some marketing to re-open for
business. All my colleagues & staff
will be there to work tomorrow.

SAMSON
Thank you for understanding Michel.

SAMIEL, SAMSON, WIFE STILL AT THE OFFICE. MICHEL LIVES THE ROOM
IS SEEN OUTSITE WALKING THE HIS CAR . . . SAM PICK UP THE PHONE . . .

SAMIEL
Steven let me have the chair,,, I am
going to have the contract changed.

SAMSON
I do not think, you can transfer the
license without the deposit. Michel
needs the money. to pay the phone
bill, F. P. L plus southern &
Spirit . . .

SAMIEL (MAD)
Samson stop it, I will take care of
those bills on credit . . . Excuse me.

SAMIEL (ON THE PHONE)
Let me speak to Mr. Borno, this is
Frank about the transfer of the
liquor license.

SECRETARY
We did fax the contract to be signed
& notarized . . . we have not received
the papers as yet . . .

SAMIEL
There is some adjustment to be made.
put Mr. borno on the phone for me
please.

SECRETARY
Please hold, he is ready for lunch.
Let me find out.

MR. BORNO
Borno, Speaking.

SAMIEL
Mr. Borno, I want you to change a
few things . . . I have just discuss
with Michel and agreed on.

BORNO
I have to go on my lunch now it's
1pm, please call me after lunch at
2pm.

SAMIEL
Please, I will be brief. We can not
wait any longer, I need to execute
the transfer as soon as possible Mr.
Borno . . .

MR. BORNO
O. k . . . Let me get a pad . . . what is the
change . . .?

SAMIEL
Everything is the same, except the
$10.000.00 deposit. we make separate
arrangement with Michel.

MR. BORNO
If I understand, no deposit to be
mentioned on the contract. transfer
the balloons payment to your name . . .
and everything else stay the same . . .

SAMIEL
Exactly, you have to transfer the
4cop to COPA TROPICAL INC. 1484 E.
Hallandale Bch. Blvd.

MR. BORNO
It is a Florida Corporation . . . Who
are the officers?

SAMIEL
President, Samson Brunachovitz . . . same

address tel: 561-654-0966.

MR BORNO
I get you Frank, I will do my best.

SAMIEL
How soon can you execute the
transfer?

MR BORNO
It takes about one week or so, from
the time Both party sign it. make
sure you send all the papers with a
check for $250.00 to Trust account
Lawrence Borno PA . . .

SAMIEL
Thank you very much . . . You have a
nice lunch . . . baa, bye.

MR. BORNO
Bye . . .

SAMSON
Dad you get it . . . we're almost there.
But how are we going to convince
Michel to sign. He need the money.

SAMIEL (LAUGHING)
The best thing is, you own a fucken
Ballroom you do not know how to
dance. Let me handle Michel . . .

SAMSON
All right . . . I am here to see what
happening, I think we get it . . . I can
also sign his name myself . . .

SAMIEL
You foolish, that will be against us
badly . . . no let me think . . . Papa Sammy
will find a way . . .

SAMSON
Michel doesn't look like a dummy
either . . .

SAMIEL (OVER THE PHONE)
Hi! Michel, this is s, s, samiel . . . I
think I have a better idea for you.
Give me a call when you get this
message. (hang up)

TRANSITION

MICHEL, DRIVING TO THE ART INSTITUTE OF FORT-LAUDERDALE . . . IS
SEEN AT WILLIAM OFFICE DISCUSSING THE DEAL WITH SAMIEL.

WILLIAM
Michel What's going on, did you give
up the whole plan? Have a seat.

MICHEL
I have nothing to worry . . . I am here
learning new trick while taking a
vacation from working for others.

WILLIAM (LAUGHING)
You such a character . . . tell me
Samuel is taking over? how is he
going to pay $15.000/month to Rock?

MICHEL
He is trying to steal my liquor
license, make some money for the
season and walk away . . .

WILLIAM (SMILLING)
So, many Evil in the World today.
Cannot get rid of them.

MICHEL
Well! We need a good attorney. I am
taking a break at School
now . . . learning for me as a teacher

is a break away from working hard.
Let talk business.

WILLIAM
I know you are on the right path . . .

MICHEL
we need to set-up a TV station on
line . . . that will promote and sell
our products . . . All the Ballroom
dance Instructional DVD' . . . create a
TV show (Education through dance)
sponsored by Arthur Murray dance
Studio

WILLIAM
Let me show you what I've done. You
are reading my mind. By the way Rock
will regret they did not give us the
Place . . . to open the college.

MICHEL
With Samuel they won't see a
penny . . . I heard they are trying to
evict him. Oh! they send me a letter
That I owed them $67.000.00 . . .

WILLIAM
what? $67.000.00. What about all
your personnel properties they took
from the facility . . . Man you need a
good lawyer . . . I have one for you.

MICHEL
I am selling the liquor license, to
pay some bills, pay my lawyer some,
to bring everybody to court.

WILLIAM
That's what you should do. Here
look, this is the site I am working
on for you . . .

Michel, William looking at the computer screen . . . A group dance choreography (Japan)

Shake William hand is seen going to his editing class . . . a film recording Studio . . . talents Video cameras . . . lots of back stage actions.

Dissolve to Michel going home . . . at the table alone having diner . . . listening to his phone messages . . . from Samuel.

MICHEL, AT THE DINING TABLE READING A BOOK . . . WALKING TO HIS BEDROOM. LAY DOWN PICK THE PHONE . . .(DIAL A NUMBER.) A LIQUOR LICENSE BROKER.

MICHEL

Mr. Garry, This is Michel from New
millennium Ballroom . . . How soon can
sell the license.

MR. GARRY

I have a buyer for a broward
license . . . I can have it done in 2 to
3 weeks . . .

MICHEL

What the value now . . .?

GARRY

Roughly! $135.000 would a fair
price . . .

MICHEL

You can go ahead sell it.

GARRY

I will prepare the package overnight
it to you to sign along with a cover
page of everything you have to get
for the transfer tomorrow by UPS . . .

MICHEL

Thank you Mr. garrison, looking
forward to your mail

EARLY MORNING, MICHEL LIVING THE HOUSE . . . IS SEEN AT THE BALLROOM
WITH SAMIEL & SAMSON

SAMIEL
I believe we have a deal, this is
all the paper from Mr. Borno, You
have to sign and I will have it
notarize and we will be in business.

SAMSON
We cannot delay any more. We just
pay Rock $20.000.00 to get the
lease . . . here is the contract sign
here.

MICHEL
I will be back! (goes to the rest
-room)

SAMSON
Dad, he won't sign it. I have that
feeling.

MICHEL (COMES BACK FROM THE RESTROOM)
Let me have the papers, my brother
have to sign it he has more share on
the license than I do . . . you need to
give a check for $10.000.00

SAMIEL
We make different arrangement. we
pay all your bills, including Rock.
We are going to pay you
$1000.00/month plus $25.000 in a
year from now. That's a good
deal . . . plus you can manage the place
as you always do . . .

MICHEL
What about my personnel &
intellectual properties . . .

SAMIEL
What properties?

SAMSON
What, What . . . I am not buying your
business . . .

MICHEL
The desk you are sitting on, the
dance floor, 3000sqf, mirror, my
daily activities I work 40 years to
put together . . . just to name a few.

SAMIEL
Anyone who would buy the business
won't have anything to do with
Ballroom Dancing. you have nothing
to sell . . .

MICHEL
We sure don't have anything to talk
about, you have a lease, the key,
and a business name . . . you ready to
go.

SAMSON
(very mad Breaking everything on
the desk.)
FUCK IT! ARE YOU GOING TO TRANSFER THE
LICENSE? THAT'S ALL I AM WORRY ABOUT.

SAMIEL
Samson,,, Samson,,, Stop this
bullshit . . . I am tired listening to
you. Let me talk to Michel, after
all I am responsible for the bills
in here no one else . . .

MICHEL
How can you folks, expect to own
everything you did not create,
without investment . . . It would be

very sad, for me to walk out here
without some sort of goodwill.

SAMIEL
I will pay all the liquor bills you
owe to the distributors. The taxes,
the phone, F. P. L . . . what else?

MICHEL
We should not argue over my
personnel properties. Leave it
between my Corporation and Rock &
associates. Let me review the
contract . . . I can make it work
without liquor license . . .

SAMSON
I want to meet with you again
tomorrow, I have someone that Might
bring some money to pay for the
license . . .

A SCENE WHERE A GROUP DANCERS KROLLING OUT EACH OTHERS FROM A
DESASTER . . . FIGHT. FADE TO MICHEL AT HIS ATTORNEY OFFICE, DANIELLA
SAGSUM PA WITH THE COURT LETTER FROM ROCK.

DANIELLA
Let me see what you get.

MICHEL
A court order, I owe $67.000.00 to
RK & Associate after the breaching
my lease agreement.

DANIELLA
This is not the proper way to do it.
this is wrong, they closed your
business without a letter of
eviction. Did the Sheriff come to
you with a Witt of eviction . . .

MICHEL

My partners and I went to renew the
lease to start in November, I gave
them the new business plan.
Everything was fine with them . . .

DANIELLA

I know this lawyer, he's a friend of
mine. this is an easy case to solve.
what do you want me to do.

MICHEL

Well in this case, I am not going
back there. they were lucky to have
a tenant like me. paying the high
rent for 8 years . . .

DANIELLA

Michel, wait a minute, let's go to
the point. They are starting a new
lease to you, you have a deposit in
their hand, the threw all your asset
in the dumpster or they took
them . . . what do you want me to do?

MICHEL

The damage is already done, my
reputation, everything is gone. how
can I face all my colleague who
believe in my work.

DANIELLA

What's the point, again, we are back
to square one. have everything
appraised, I need a value of your
lost . . . plus you need to consider
attorney fees . . . the economy is bad
for everyone . . .

MICHEL

32 boxes full with all my research
papers, my movies scripts, my Dance

instructional DVD Scripts, music,
books, liquor, all my files. all
gone . . . Money cannot buy all these.
how can I appraise them. they are
gone . . .40 years of all my
accumulated knowledge and saving are
invested in the facility . . .

DANIELLA
Again, If I were you, I would go
back change the lock and re-open.
your lease is not expires until
October 31, 2008. the change the
lock on you in September . . .

MICHEL
You can start work on filing back to
the court. I am selling the liquor
license, so I can pay you something
from what I owe you.

DANIELLA
It's been a while, I have to
calculate how much.

MICHEL
Thank you Dan . . . I will make an
estimate Value of my lost.

DANIELLA
Very good, here a list of what I
need from you . . . see you . . . you still
can work with the new guy, he gave
you a key . . . make some money at least
to live.

MICHEL
I have a few private lessons, I
will. good day Daniela. Bye.

DANIELLA
Bye . . .

A SCENE WHERE GOD RETURN TO CHANGE NATURE . . . MUSICAL SCENE.
(VERY MAD) AND GO.
FADE TO
MICHEL LEAVES IN HIS CAR . . . GO TO THE BALLROOM WITH MATTHEW &
MILLIE . . . TWO OF HIS TRAINEES TO MANAGE THE BALLROOM FOR SAM.
THEY WERE SITTING AT THE BALLROOM WAITING FOR MICHEL . . .

                              MICHEL
                   Samuel, while we are undecided on
                       some stuffs. Here is Matthew and
                     Millie, this couple are well train
                    to manage when I am not here. Next
                   week I have to go back to work in
                   Japan . . . I will come back within 2
                              weeks.

                              SAMIEL
                   What your name Millae, and you are?

                              John
                     John . . . Tindal . . .(Laughing very
                    funny) I am from Trinidad, Millie is
                            from Peru

                              SAMIEL
                       Millie, Te habla espanol?

                              Marian
                    Si . . . si nosotros studentes del
                          maestro Michel . . .

                              John
                   We love the place, and love to see
                   you succeed and that is why we are
                            here to help.

MICHEL SAY GOOD BYE TO SAMIEL, MILLIE AND MATTHEW . . . WENT TO
PICK UP VERONICA FOR RESEARSING AT THE BALLROOM LATER. THEY WENT
TO MAMAMIA RESTAURENT WITH DOMINIQUE AND HERBY . . . LATER ON
DR. FANFAN SHOWS UP TO THE RESTAURENT . . .

They all are eating and see each others living the restaurent . . . V. O all conversation.

Dr. Fanfan, Dominique and Herby are hugging Michel & Veronica wishing them a nice trip to Japan . . .

DR. FANFAN
Guys next time I will go to asia
with you . . . I Love asian.

DOMINIQUE
We all will make a trip together.
Bye Dr. Fanfan . . .

HERBY, DOMINIQUE, VERONICA AND MICHEL IN THE SAME CAR LIVING. DR. FANFAN IS SEEN LIVING THE PACKING LOT IN HIS CONVERTIBLE MERCEDES BEND.

TRANSITION

Veronica and Michel is seen at the Ballroom rehearsing a beautiful Viennese waltz choreography . . .
Left for Japan . . . Michel & Veronica back stage in the Dressing room in Japan Theatre, getting ready to perform . . .
MANY JAPONESE KIDS FROM ERIKA'S BALLET SCHOOL ARE ON STAGE PERFORMING FOLLOWED BY COUPLE DANCING BALLET CLASSIC, MICHEL AND VERONICA IS DANCING A BEAUTIFUL AMERICAN FOX-TROT BROADWAY STYLE, BELLY DANCERS FROM GREECE . . . PERFORM A BELLY DANCE ROUTINE.

(Grand Finally Erika's 12
minutes Choreography a
formation team Show The poem
of the earth)
CREDITS . . .
FADE TO BLACK
THE END

BASED ON A TRUE STORY!
By: Michel F. Jacques

(New Millennium Ballroom College tv.)

To Boost the idea . . . Dance Medicine & Science

If you search the Global Dance Directory using "therapy" as keyword you get 2600 listings. This means that approximately one in every hundred dance professionals provides some form of therapy. Though 0.01% is a very small percentage, therapy is probably the most rapidly expanding branch of the dance industry. The proliferation of courses and workshops shows that the number of dance therapists has the potential to double every year. Qualified professionals are increasingly employed in hospitals, health centers, aged persons' homes, prisons or mental asylums. Private practices are multiplying, and so are conventional dance schools offering therapy classes.

This boom might be due to the fact that curing through dance comes under the Ministry of Health in many countries, so the possibility of funding is incomparably higher than when dance is oriented towards performance or recreation. Another reason is that, since our modern way of life has alienated man from primary functions, people are rediscovering the power of dance to heal.

Dancing certainly makes a healthy person feel better, but seeking to alleviate a manifest psychological problem through dance is another thing. Traditional societies have preserved well-being by providing frequent opportunities to dance in social gatherings and in rituals. Since these events have been abandoned our frustration has accumulated, so now we turn to sessions by professionals to satisfy that need. Specific dances have been used to cure some illnesses - research is required to find out if those dances can be used today for the same purpose.

Even more impressive is the fact that patients have been cured not by their own dancing but by the dancing of another person. In many countries of the world people ask healers, shamans and witch-doctors to continue age-old practices because they find them beneficial. These dances, rejected so far by industrialized societies, deserve serious study.

Modern dance therapy, though only a few decades old, has developed new techniques, only partially based on traditional practices. It produces a body of knowledge, theoretical as well as applied, and establishes its effectiveness. Much more needs to be done.
This is starting right here in the USA

What I want to do for peace, is to share my knowledge of Music & Dance with the coming generation. Music & dance are special Languages, and I think Music & Dance together can communication things that are difficult to communicate with words. Specially things that are related to emotion we, have to share as human being. There is always and forever the joy in the music and the dance. For the past 30 years I have thought and dance with people who cannot communicate with words, I believe this is a first step for different ethnic community to communicate and work toward peace.

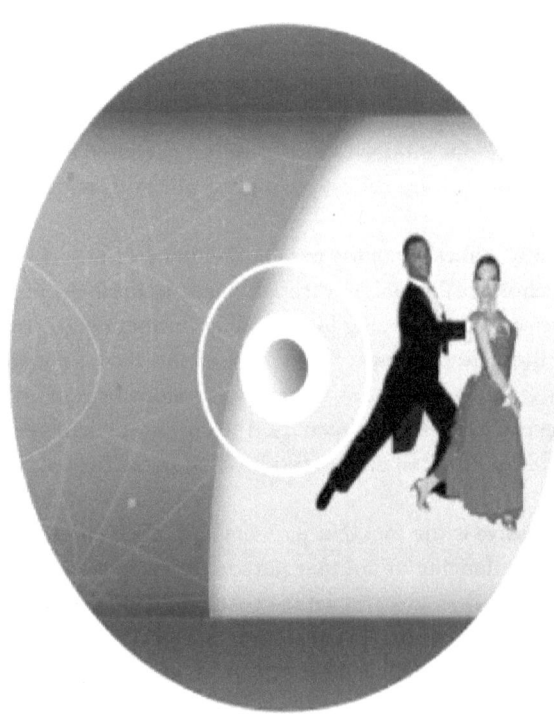

Base on a true will be in theatre near you

New Millennium Ballroom Business Review

This Business Review, presented by Valu-Edge Consulting LLC, is intended to acquaint a prospective **Investor** with relevant preliminary information regarding New Millennium Ballroom, a d/b/a of Le Creole Productions, Inc., (hereinafter "The Company" or "New Millennium Ballroom") whose business is currently available for acquisition, sale or merger. The overall format of this Confidential Business Review is designed to reflect a prospective Investor/purchaser the factors that create value within the Company and assumes that any sale will take the form of either the sale of assets with assumption of operating liabilities or the sale of stock. The plan you are about to review was given to the landlord, city official, Copa Tropical Inc and other colleagues with interest in taking over the lease promises.

TABLE OF CONTENTS

COMPANY PROFILE

Background: New Millennium Ballroom is a Florida S Corporation. The Company is a private ballroom dance instruction and video production studio. The Company was established in 1997, and has been under current management since inception. New Millennium Ballroom is located at 1484 E. Hallandale Beach Blvd., Hallandale Beach, Florida, **33009**. As of fiscal year ending 2006, the Company generated total revenues of $510,958.

According to management, New Millennium Ballroom has earned an excellent reputation over the past 13 years for its expedient and reliable service, expertise in the industry, skilled and experienced staff, prompt response time, convenient hours and location, and competitive prices. The Company maintains an extensive base of accounts, throughout Broward County, Hallandale Beach, and surrounding communities.

Hallandale Beach is located in the far southeast region of Florida, and approximately 399 miles from Tallahassee the state capital. A summary of relevant information includes:

- ❑ The population of Hallandale Beach is approximately 35,369.
- ❑ The approximate number of housing units is 18,051.
- ❑ The amount of land area in Hallandale is 4 square miles.
- ❑ The amount of surface water is 0.34 square miles.
- ❑ Hallandale is positioned 25.98 degrees north of the equator and 80.14 degrees west of the prime meridian.

Products and Services: New Millennium Ballroom is a reputable and well established ballroom and video production studio. New Millennium Ballroom's objective is to create better performing artists, dancers, musicians and film actors in the entertainment industry. The program will begin teaching dance from elementary school to university level helping create the dance professional of the future. In the domestic and international community, there is a constant need for performing artists (models, choreographers, musicians, actors, etc.). The youth will be able to use their talent, natural ability and the knowledge of the fundamental schooling in their careers.

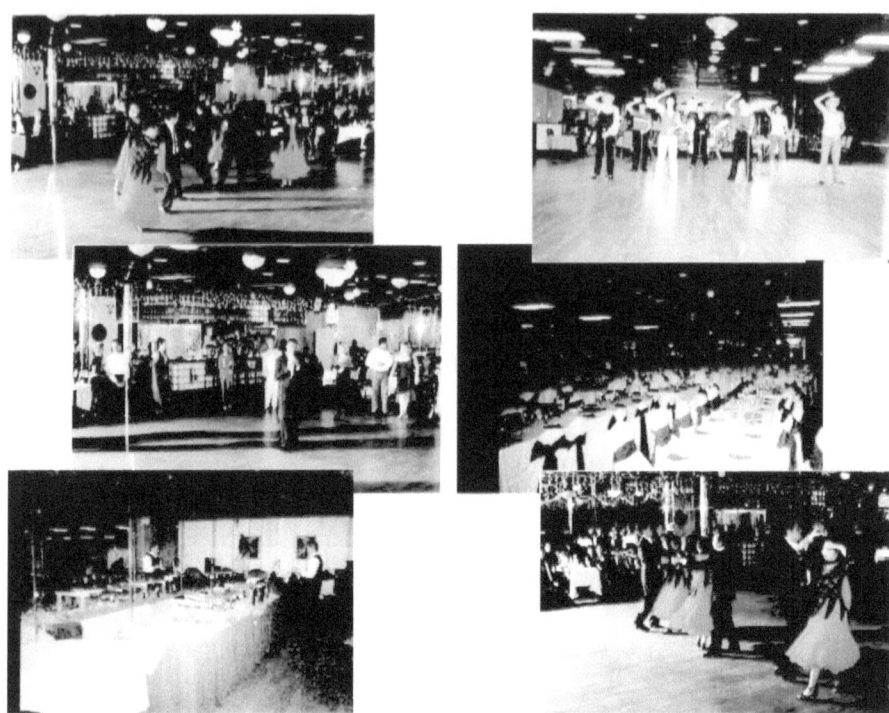

New Millennium Ballroom was in operation seven days a week. The Company was an owner-operated business, and operated from a leased remodeled single level building in good overall condition, approximately 7,000 square feet in size. The site of operations is in a large shopping center located on a downtown city street by an interstate state highway which provides high traffic and good visibility. The Company website is **www.millenniumballroom.net.**

New Millennium Ballroom strives to be the only organization to create and manage high performing artists in the industry of film and cinema as well as world class ballroom dance competitors.

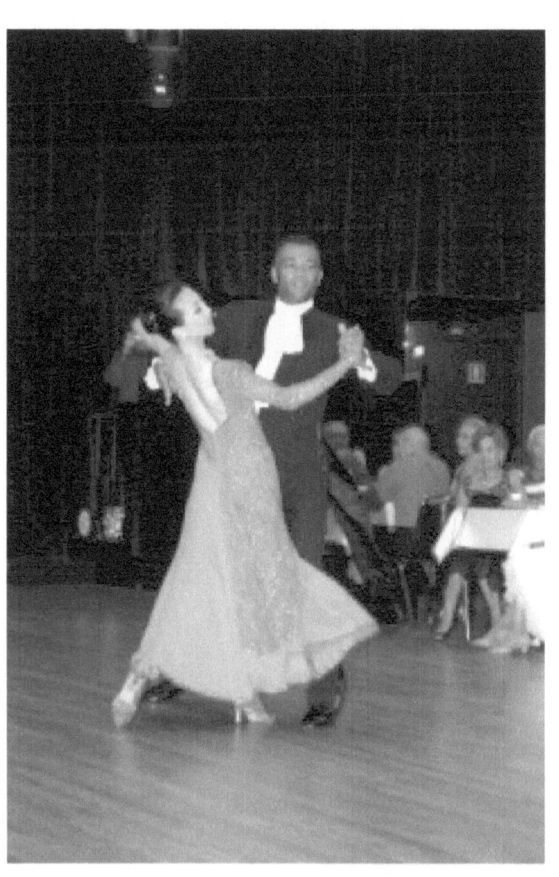

Goals:

I.   Will design and develop a daily dance program for local and seasonal residents, students and members via our dance halls and studios, the New Millennium Ballroom and affiliated studios in the South Miami area.

II. Will produce a unique television program to promote and sell our products, video/DVD dance instructional, music, film and documentaries generating enough profit to enable a fair return for finance, continued growth and development in quality products in the music and film industry.

III. Maintain a friendly, fair and creative work environment, respect diversity, support a professional work ethic and foster the new ideas through R&D program.

IV. Stimulate health education and career opportunities through university and college academic research and partnership with school of arts and family therapy, etc.

Keys to success:

To work hand to hand with all professional dance teachers' active members of the New Millennium Ballroom club/CID to form a committee responsible for training, coaching and teaching in both private and public schools.

Worldwide preparation for dance teacher's certification will also be provided for international expansion.

In addition, the Company will:

❑ Achieve a minimum net profit in the range of 20% to 30% on sales of Educational programming, dance lessons and parties.

❑ Provide better ways to promote diversity. Maintain gross margin level at or above 60%.

Market: **New Millennium Ballroom** maintains an extensive base of satisfied accounts with a moderate amount of advertising. According to management there is a low level of local competition to the business. Name recognition, honesty, integrity, quality of workmanship, reputation, longevity, established patronage and diversity are attributes that are associated with this company.

Management: Management is primarily provided by the owner and is an owner-operated business. The Company maintains a knowledgeable staff. The Company's management team consists of seasoned managers and experts in the field of teaching whose background and experience make them ideally suited to their roles. The owner will remain for a period of time, if so desired by buyer, to ensure a smooth transition, with time allotment and compensation to be determined.

Equipment: All of **New Millennium Ballroom's** assets are available for purchase with the business. The equipment is leading edge and is in excellent condition. No independent appraisal on the assets, being sold with the business, has been performed by Valu-Edge Consulting, LLC or National Business Capital Services, LLC.

Local Demographics: Hallandale Beach is located in Broward County, which has a population of 1,787,636 (2005 U.S. Census Estimate), and 790,308 housing units. The population density of Broward County is persons per square mile.

From April 1, 2000 to July 1, 2005, the population of Broward County increased by 10.1%, compared to 13.2% for the state of Florida, and 6.4% for the United States.

Broward County has a median household income of $43,136 and a per capita income of $23,170, compared to a median household income of $40,900 and a per capita income of $21,557 for the state of Florida. The median household income for the United States is $44,334 and the per capita income is $21,587.

The home ownership rate for Broward County is 69.5%, with the median value of owner-occupied homes being $128,600. The state of Florida has a home ownership rate of 70.1%, with a median value of $105,500, while the United States has a 66.2% ownership rate with a median value of $119,600.

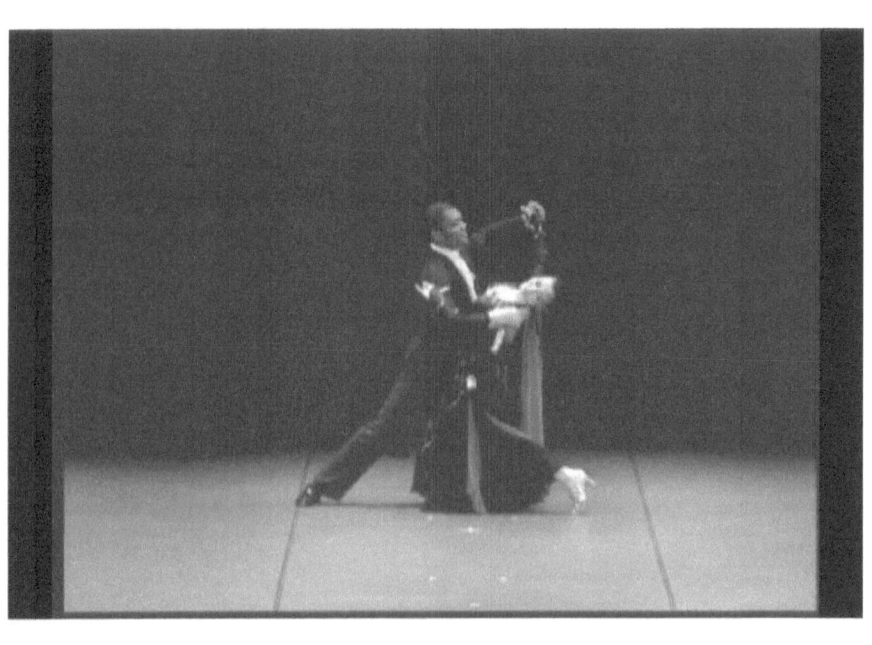

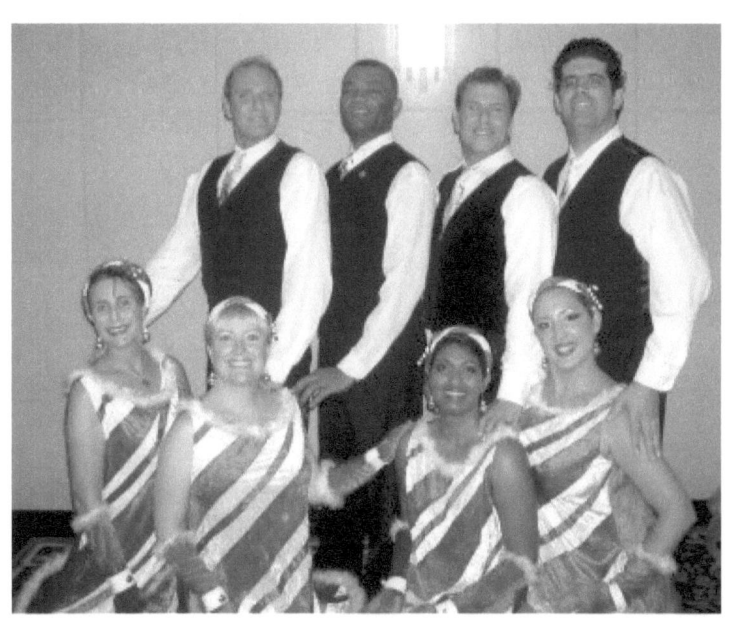

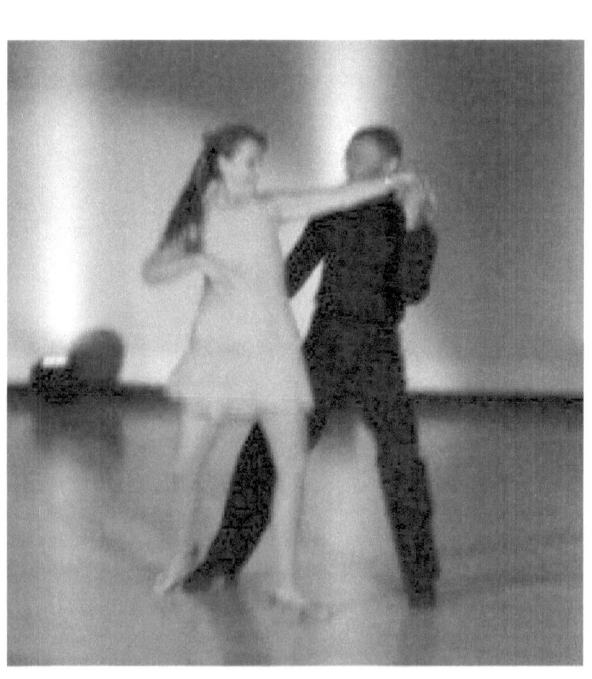

INDUSTRY OVERVIEW

Economic Outlook through 2010: The following is a summary of economic predictions from 2004 to 2010, released by the Bureau of Labor Statistics (BLS).

The BLS predicts economic growth with high productivity, low unemployment, and strong exports. The nation's gross domestic product (GDP) is expected to reach $12.8 trillion by the end of the decade, and increase of $3.6 trillion from 2000. GDP is expected to grow at an average annual rate of 3.4%. It grew by 3.2% from 1999 to 2000.

However, despite the higher GDP growth rate, the BLS estimates that employment growth from 2004 to 2010 will be slightly lower than it was in the previous decade. Civilian household employment is likely to grow 1.1% annually from 2004 to 2010, while it increased by 1.3% a year from 1990 to 2000. The report assumes 4% unemployment for 2010, the same rate in 2000.

Personal consumption spending which accounts for two-thirds of all economic activity is expected to grow at an average annual rate of 3.5% from 2004 to 2010, versus 3.4% from 1990 to 2000.

The BLS anticipates that spending on durable consumer goods will grow at an average annual rate of 5% through 2010. The following areas should see particular growth:

- ❑ *Motor vehicles:* Spending on light vehicles (small pickup trucks, sport utility vehicles, and mini vans) is expected to increase 3.5% annually to 2010. This is down from the 7.9% increase in consumer spending on light vehicles from 1995 to 2000. The demand for automobiles is expected to ease, but remain strong.
- ❑ *Personal computers:* From 2004 to 2010, spending on personal computers will probably increase 22% annually, fueled by competition between computer manufacturers, declining prices, and increased use of the Internet. By 2010, consumers will lay out $802.4 billion on computers, up from $108.8 billion in 2000.
- ❑ *Software:* A 7.4% yearly increase in consumer spending on software is forecast from 2004 to 2010. Spending should reach $36.3 billion in 2010, up from $17.8 billion in 2000 and $500 million in 1990.
- ❑ *Furniture:* Personal expenditures on furniture are projected to increase 5.1% annually to 2010, down slightly from the 6.3% annual increase from 1990 to 2000.
- ❑ *Eyewear:* Increasing disposable income and an older population are predicted to increase demand for eyeglasses and contact lenses by 3.1% a year from 2004 to 2010, compared with 2.4% during the previous decade.

Spending on non-durable consumer goods is expected to rise, but at a slower pace than on durable goods.

- ❑ *Food and clothing:* Expenditures on food and beverages are projected to increase 2.3% from 2004 to 2010, 0.3% faster than from 1990 to 2000. Demand for bottled water and convenience foods have increased in recent years. A 4.3% annual growth rate is forecast for shoes and clothing from 2000 to 2010, down from 5.5% between 1990 and 2000, and 4.7% from 1980 to 1990.
- ❑ *Gasoline and fuel oil:* Personal consumption on gasoline and motor oil is expected to rise by 2.2% each year from 2004 and 2010. Expenditures on fuel oil and coal are likely to increase 1.1% annually. The price of imported oil is projected to decline slightly, encouraging consumption.
- ❑ *Drugs and medicine:* Demand for drugs and medicine is growing rapidly. The aging population and a rising standard of living will prompt an 8.5% annual increase in personal spending on drugs and medicine between 2004 and 2010, compared with 5.7% from 1990 to 2000.
- ❑ *Consumer services:* Spending on consumer's services, including housing and medical care, will likely increase 3.1% annually from 2004 to 2010. This category represents more than half of all consumption and constitutes one-third of real GDP.
- ❑ *Housing and household operation:* Household formation will probably expand 1.1% annually from 2004 to 2010. Telephone service is expected to grow 7.6% annually due to increasing numbers of telephone lines per household and the use of cellular phones.
- ❑ *Medical services:* A 2.7% annual increase in the consumption of medical services from 2004 to 2010 is forecast.
- ❑ *Recreation services and personal business services:* Reflecting a rise in incomes, spending on recreational services is predicted to rise 6% each year from 2004 to 2010. Personal business services (investment counseling, legal advice, and accounting) should expand 3.2% annually through 2010.

The business investment category, which includes residential structures, will likely increase 6.2% per year from 2004 to 2010.

- ❑ *Business computers:* Demand for business computers is expected to grow 15.2% annually between 2004 and 2010, due to declining prices, technological advances, and the development of global information infrastructures. Spending on business computers grew by 35.2% annually between 1990 and 2000.
- ❑ *Software:* Business investment in software is projected to grow 12.6% each year through 2010, down from the 15.1% annual increase in the previous

decade. The spread of electronic commerce and new products, such as web page design, are fueling demand.

❏ *Communication equipment*: Technological advances, such as the development of wireless equipment, are generating strong growth in communications equipment, and 4.5% annual growth through 2010 is anticipated.

❏ *Nonresidential structures*: The BLS projects a 1.9% yearly increase in nonresidential construction from 2000 to 2010. Annual growth predictions for subcategories are: buildings and other structures, 2.3%; mining and exploration, 1.1%; and public utilities, 0.4%.

❏ *Fixed residential structures*: Investment in residential structures will probably grow at 2.3% annually to 2010, down from 3.9% in the 1990s. There are fewer people in the prime home buying group, age 35 to 44.

International trade is expected to account for an ever increasing share of GDP. In 1980, exports were 6.8% of GDP, rising to 8.6% in 1990 and 12.3% in 2000. Imports accounted for 6.7% of GDP in 1980, swelling to 9.4% in 1990 and 16.6% in 2000.

Imports have continued to outpace exports, increasing the US trade deficit from $56.5 billion in 1990 to $399.1 billion in 2000 and a projected $889.1 billion in 2010. However, the BLS points out those cheaper imports have also helped in the US economy by keeping inflation low and boosting consumer spending.

From 2004 to 2010, exports are expected to grow 7.8% annually, versus 7% during the previous decade, while imports are projected to increase 7.9%.

❏ *Exports of goods*: According to the report, the largest export growth will be in computers, with demand increasing at an anticipated 16.8% annually from 2004 to 2010. The market for telecommunications equipment should also be strong.

❏ *Exports of services*: Globalization will spur business needs for communications, insurance, and financial services. This category is expected to grow at 7.1% each year between 2004 and 2010.

❏ *Imports of goods*: Since the international computer market is highly competitive, computers represent a fast-growing import, as well as export, category. Demand for foreign-made computers is expected to remain strong through 2010, growing at a rate of 15.9%. Petroleum is likely to account for an even larger share of imports, increasing at 1.2% each year, as domestic production declines.

❏ *Imports to services*: In response to greater globalization, US companies are expected to seek more professional services in foreign markets, boosting demand by 4.9% each year from 2004 to 2010.

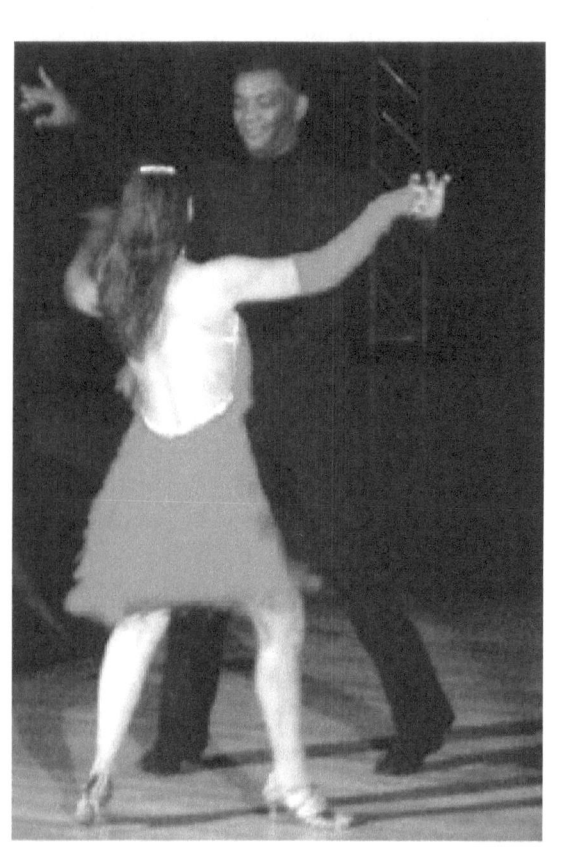

FINANCIAL INFORMATION AND ANALYSIS

Financial Statement Presentation: The financial information presented is utilized in analyzing the financial position of the Company.

The Company's financial statements are reported by the Company's management and other accountants. These reported historical financial statements are included solely to assist the reader of this report, and they should not be used to obtain credit or for any other purpose. Because of the limited purpose of these presentations, they may be incomplete and contain departures from generally accepted accounting principles. Valu-Edge Consulting LLC has not audited, reviewed, or compiled these presentations and expresses no assurance on them.

The exhibits as presented are:

1) Exhibit A-1 represents the Company's reported "Condensed Income Sheets—As Reported" as prepared by management and/or other accountants for the fiscal years ending December 31, 2004 through 2006.
2) Exhibit A-2 represents the "Condensed Income Statements—Adjustments" to the Company's reported income statements to more accurately reflect the potential return to an investor for the fiscal years ending December 31, 2004 through 2006. For analysis purposes, adjustments were made for deferred revenue and discretionary expenses.
3) Exhibit A-3 represents the "Condensed Income Statement—As Adjusted" of the Company which more equitably reflects the potential return to an investor for the fiscal years ending December 31, 2004 through 2006.
4) Exhibit A-4 represents the "Condensed Income Statements—Common Size (% of Net Revenues)" of the Company. This statement is analyzed to identify the trends among the various periods and the relationships within each of the periods.
5) Exhibit A-5 represents the "Condensed Income Statements—Change Versus Prior Period" of the Company. This statement is analyzed to identify the trends among the various periods and the relationships within each of the periods.
6) Exhibit B-1 represents the "Operating Financial Analysis—Selected Performance Ratios" of the Company. This statement is analyzed to identify the trends among the various periods and the relationships within each of the periods.

General Income Statement Observations: Exhibits A-1 through A-5 contain **New Millennium Ballroom's** income statement data for the fiscal years ending December

31, 2004 through 2006. The income statement reflects the results of operations over a period of time.

Generally, past sales and earnings growth can indicate future growth and can place the entity's current performance in a historical context. Other things being equal, a company with rapidly rising sales and earnings is worth more than one with little or no growth.

Adjusted financial statements assist in accessing the firm's future on-going earning power and the risk of the cash flows associated with operations. Generally, these adjustments:

1. Provide a consistent and reasonable starting point to begin the analysis process. These adjustments are typically categorized as departures from Generally Accepted Accounting Principles (GAAP).
2. Provide consistency from period to period in order to assess expected future performance. These adjustments are typically to transactions, which under normal circumstances are not expected to occur in the future (e.g. nonrecurring items, extraordinary items).

The adjusted income statements are utilized for financial analysis purposes only. Normalization adjustments are hypothetical in nature and are not intended to restate historical results in accordance with American Institute of Certified Public Accountants (AICPA) guidelines.

During the period under review New Millennium Ballroom's adjusted revenues have increased from $259,740 in FYE 2004 to $570,958 in FYE 2006. This represents a compound annual growth rate of 30.0 percent and a three-year period-to-period average of 51.9 percent. In FYE 2006, adjusted revenues increased 84.9 percent to $570,958.

The Company's cost of sales as a percentage of sales has ranged from a low of 18.5 percent in FYE 2004 to a high of 38.8 percent in FYE 2006. The cost of sales period-to-period three-year average is 25.4 percent of sales. In FYE 2006 cost of sales was 38.8 percent reaching $221,470.

The Company's operating expenses as a percentage of sales has ranged from a low of 41.7 percent in FYE 2006 to a high of 62.7 percent in FYE 2004 and has averaged 55.4 percent from FYE 2004 through FYE 2006.

In FYE 2006 operating expenses was 41.7 percent of revenues and amounted to $238,078.

The Company's operating profits as a percentage of sales has ranged from a low of 18.7 percent in FYE 2004 to a high of 19.5 percent in FYE 2006 and has averaged 19.2 percent from FYE 2004 through FYE 2006. During FYE 2006, operating profits were 19.5 percent of revenues and equaled $111,410.

The Company's operating profits as a percentage of sales were 19.5 percent in FYE 2006. During FYE 2006 revenues equaled $570,958.

Operating profits increased from 19.4 percent in FYE 2005 to 19.5 percent in FYE 2006 and were above the three year average of 19.2 percent.

Internal and Comparative Ratio Analysis: Exhibit B-1 illustrates some of the pertinent financial ratios for the Company from December 31, 2004 through 2006.

The ratios have been classified into the principle category of operating profitability. This category emphasizes different relationships within the entity and allows for a comparative analysis of entity's operating in a similar type of business. The comparative analysis is performed by utilizing industry statistics from Risk Management Association (RMA).

Operating profitability ratios typically indicate the ability of a company in the utilization of its assets, management, and liabilities to maximize revenues while minimizing expenses. Generally, the profitability ratios agree with the findings discussed within the income statement section.

❏ Gross Profit Margin (Gross Profit divided by Sales)—The Company's gross profit margin has ranged from 61.2 percent to 81.5 percent and has averaged 74.6 percent over the periods analyzed. As of FYE 2006 the Company's gross profit margin was 61.2 percent.

❏ Operating Profit Margin—The Company's operating profit margin has ranged from 18.7 percent to 19.5 percent and has averaged 19.2 percent over the periods analyzed. As of FYE 2006 the Company's operating profit margin was 19.5 percent.

❏ Pre-Tax Profit Margin—The Company's pre-tax profit margin has ranged from 16.3 percent to 18.0 percent and has averaged 17.3 percent over the periods analyzed. As of FYE 2006 the Company's pre-tax profit margin was 17.5 percent.

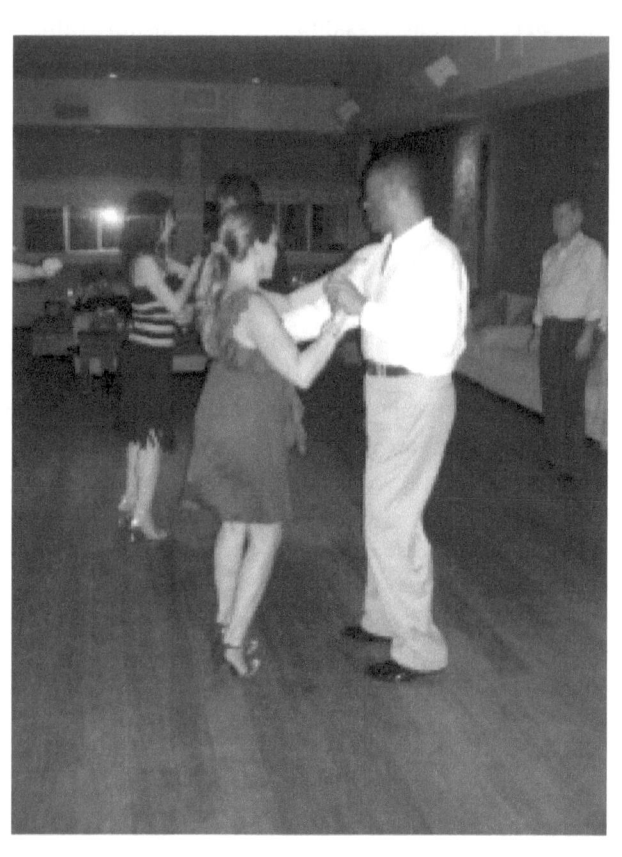

STRATEGIC ENHANCEMENT OPPORTUNITIES

Introduction: New Millennium Ballroom has positioned itself to grow to the next level. According to management, the future of this company includes:

❑ Strong growth potential due to increases in both local and regional populations, and forecasted increases in consumer spending.

❑ Increase revenues through investors and partnering with the city to increase cash flow, expanding to other cities, and increasing marketing and promotion efforts.

❑ Maintain loyal and consistent customers that continually provide "word-of-mouth" advertising.

❑ Continued profitability and profit margins.

❑ Leading edge and well maintained equipment.

❑ Increased visibility in the fine arts schools market.

The Future: A more aggressive marketing campaign would have a significant impact on revenue growth for New Millennium Ballroom. An ideal marketing program would include a moderate increase in print advertising, enhancement and comprehensive utilization of the existing company website, and creating additional strategic partnering relationships.

Although these strategic plans do take time to implement, the first focus of a new buyer should be on increasing the services the company currently offers. A forecasted income statement covering the next five years is presented on the following page. The first and second forecasted years assume conservative growth rates, while successive years reflect expansion through the successful implementation of the strategic plan offered in this report.

Over the forecasted period, the Company's operating profile is expected to be:

Earnings Measure Summary	Profile
Revenues	100.00%
EBITDA* Owner's Comp.	21.00%
EBITDA*	21.00%
EBIT**	21.00%
Net Income	18.99%

*Earnings before interest, taxes, depreciation/amortization. **Earnings before interest, and taxes.

A new energetic buyer is expected to grow the business significantly and is expected to experience a learning curve during the first year of operations. The forecasted income statement for New Millennium Ballroom is:

	Base Yr 2006 ($)	Five Yr Growth				
		Forecasted Yr 1 Revenue Growth of 59% ($)	Forecasted Yr 2 Revenue Growth of 54% ($)	Forecasted Yr 3 Revenue Growth of 49% ($)	Forecasted Yr 4 Revenue Growth of 44% ($)	Forecasted Yr 5 Revenue Growth of 39% ($)
Net Revenues	570,958	907,823	1,398,048	2,083,091	2,999,651	4,169,515
Less Cost of Sales	221,470	344,973	531,258	791,575	1,139,867	1,584,416
Gross Profit	349,488	562,850	866,790	1,291,517	1,859,784	2,585,099
Direct Operating Expenses (excl. Interest)	238,078	372,208	573,200	854,067	1,229,857	1,709,501
ESOP Contribution	0	0	0	0	0	0
Operating Profit	111,410	190,643	293,590	437,449	629,927	875,598
Non-operating Income/Expense	0	0	0	0	0	0
Interest Expense	-11,482	-18,256	-28,115	-41,891	-60,323	-83,849
Pre-Tax Profit	99,928	172,386	265,475	395,558	569,604	791,749
Less Income Taxes	0	0	0	0	0	0
Net Income Before Extraordinary Income (Expense)	99,928	172,386	265,475	395,558	569,604	791,749
Extraordinary Income (Expense)	0	0	0	0	0	0
Net Income Before Preferred Divs	99,928	172,386	265,475	395,558	569,604	791,749
Preferred Dividends Paid	0	0	0	0	0	0
Adjusted Net Income Available To Common Shareholders	99,928	172,386	265,475	395,558	569,604	791,749
Discretionary Cash Flow (Net Profit Attributable to Common Shareholders Before Extra Items + Depreciation)	99,928	172,386	265,475	395,558	569,604	791,749
Earnings Per Common Share (Before Extraordinary Items)	99,928	172,386	265,475	395,558	569,604	791,749
Cash Flow Per Common Share	99,928	172,386	265,475	395,558	569,604	791,749
Depr. & Amort. Expense	0	0	0	0	0	0
Lease & Rental Expense	150,840	150,840	150,840	150,840	150,840	150,840
Annual Interest Expense	11,482	18,256	28,115	41,891	60,323	83,849
Non Operating Income	0	0	0	0	0	0
Profit Sharing Contribution	0	0	0	0	0	0
Common Dividends Paid	0	0	0	0	0	0
Officer Compensation	0	0	0	0	0	0
Shares Outstanding						
Common Shares	1	1	1	1	1	1
Less Treas. Shares	0	0	0	0	0	0
Year-End Shares Outstanding	1	1	1	1	1	1
Mean or Avg. Shares	1	1	1	1	1	1
Preferred Shares Outstanding	0	0	0	0	0	0
Earning Measure Summary						
Revenues	570,958	907,823	1,398,048	2,083,091	2,999,651	4,169,515
Gross Income & Owner's Comp	111,410	190,643	293,590	437,449	629,927	875,598
Gross Income	111,410	190,643	293,590	437,449	629,927	875,598
Operating Income	111,410	190,643	293,590	437,449	629,927	875,598
Net Income	99,928	172,386	265,475	395,558	569,604	791,749

The Principle of Future Benefits considers the "potential earning capacity" of a business. The method used to consider this aspect is the Discounted Future Benefits Method. Founded on the principle of future benefits, the value of a business is the present value of all the "benefits" it can reasonably be expected to generate in the future. These "benefits" are generally considered to be the future cash flows available to the owners from the business.

Discounted Future Benefits Method
100% Control Interest -- Equity Valued Directly

Year	Forecasted Cash Flow		46% Present Value Factors		Present Value Future Cash Flow
1st Year	190,643	x	0.68493	=	130,577
2nd Year	293,590	x	0.46913	=	137,732
3rd Year	437,449	x	0.32132	=	140,561
4th Year	629,927	x	0.22008	=	138,634
5th Year	875,598	x	0.15074	=	131,988
Terminal Value	2,097,363	x	0.15074	=	316,156
Total Indicated Value					995,648

Terminal Value:

Fifth Year	875,598	x	1.03	=	901,866	=	2,097,363
					43.0%		

Total Indicated Value - Rounded		**996,000**
Add / Less: Net Assets (Excluding Fixed Assets) and Liabilities Expected to Transfer		-
Estimated Operating Value of Asset Sale		**996,000**
Add / Less: Estimated Value of Other Assets/Liabilities		0
Estimated Value of Asset Sale		**996,000**
	Round	**996,000**

Using New Millennium Ballroom's forecasted cash flows the Discounted Future Benefits Method can be used to establish a present value associated with anticipated future revenue.

Conclusion: New Millennium Ballroom is now known as **NATIONAL DANCE COUNCIL HAITI INC.** a Florida S Corporation. The Company is a private ballroom dance instruction and video/film production studio. As of fiscal year ending 2006, the Company generated total revenues of $510,958.

The National Dance Council Haiti Inc. is expected to provide future economic benefits of $996,000. Future economic benefits plus expected asset transfers are valued at $996,000.

The Company has experienced a consistent demand for its services due to satisfied customer referrals and dependable quality. There is no doubt that this trend can be continued into the future.

Should a new owner follow the successful business strategy developed by the current owner, including the "Strategic Enhancement Opportunities" discussed earlier, this business should be able to experience a tremendous amount of future growth in both revenue and profits. The continued success of this business, in light of recent national economic developments, is largely dependent on the expertise of management.

APPENDIX

Dr. Goldsmith Dorval in his book, (Quand la Musique Parle aux Hommes) undertakes an analytic essay, historical, educational, and therapeutic. He exposed different styles of music and their therapeutic value. He emphasizes on voodoo music how it's been neglected. (My feeling is perhaps it has been misinterpreted). "The importance of voice in oral communication in our therapeutic effort in daily life put into the public disposal as a means of self-cure". Music is constructed for many reasons, mainly to control our emotional filters. The role of music for me, back then, was a true essay of vulgarization. The way music is made can either be therapeutic, or it can also be very destructive to the mind settings.

Translated from Dr. Dorval book "The blacks from Africa didn't have a written language to communicate. They brought with them music and dance as the most precious products they could give to the island. For them, Music and Dance transforms life into energy to light up the environment. A dancer's posture can change the meaning of the dance. A curving action of the upper back can be interpreted as a dance of supplication with hands on the knee. The movement of the snake is a symbol of Damballah, the god of love. The tide's movement has to do with Agoe the god of the sea". The knees, shoulders, and every part of the human body can be used to express something specific in a more spiritual level.

Samba, Congo, and Compas are all considered the dance of joy that can lead us to the height of ecstasy. The dresses, the makeup, the excitement of all movements give a sense of eternal life. Brazil, Haiti, and Mexico are considered originators of dance cultural activities. They dance ibo in honor of the spirit of all their ancestors who died from slavery. Petro dances develop a sense of dominance of the world as it is usually different from the way other dancers see it. These people tend to be very violent and aggressive; their favorite color is usually red. It is a custom of living developed in the island of Saint-Domingue.

Nago, Banda, is not always about steps or footwork like the toe, ball, heel in ballroom dancing, it is emotion that controls the actions. It is a traditional style of philosophy. For most traditional dancers, death is nonexistent. They refuse to believe that there is an end to life, more sex is a message of regeneration hence, and voodoo is attributed to a theatrical function for these practitioners. The newer Haitian social dance art form is the kompa; it is usually danced in the dark, purely for safe sex. The social concept of dance my partner Fong and I presented in 2005, in Lanarca, Cyprus, to the international congress was a promotion to a new concept of dancing the kompa. We believe that talents cannot develop without skills. We can create a new Haitian identity by the way we dance the kompa.

My choreographies are slightly different; first, they are self-made. I developed the skill in listening to a beautiful piece of a musical. I sense some sort of inspiration from the singer's tone of voice, which helps in the creation of inspirational movements. Usually, that's all I need in combination with school figures to create a nice show. I sometimes listen instead to other instruments, search for other musicians' inspirations, and do the same, while staying within the characterization of the dance. It is more enjoyable and therapeutic for me to dance that way.

When I learn with a coach, I find they stress more on psychology and modeling which limits me from expressing my true emotions. I try not to become a photocopy of someone else. I love to share my thoughts and creativities with all my students and colleagues. Giving to the students what they need and teaching to their abilities for me is a human act.

My home town:

Les Cayes, if I remember, in 1503, was under the rule of Nicolas de Ovando, the representative of Spain, after Christopher Columbus. In time they decided to build cities, which required them to bring into Haiti top engineers, who searched for a place suitable enough to hold the desired construction. They ended up choosing Les Cayes. Les Cayes, has a perfect architectural land base. There are no mountains. The flat land made it easier for the architects and engineers to design a modern city. Les Cayes was built mainly for international partners and as a tourist attraction. Every street, you look down, has a beach view at the far end of it. Les Cayes is surrounded by flowing rivers, which serve as inter-coastal waterways.

Today in Les Cayes, more than a hundred years later, a few centennial houses are still standing, along with the paved roads that were built. Deterioration has taken over the antiquity of this beautiful city. Architects have recently built a few more houses but due to the huge difference in education from then and now, these houses had to be rebuilt after just a few years because they were breaking down.

Outside of Les Cayes were the people that lived on the countryside of Haiti who worked in the sugarcane fields. They would often go to Cuba on weekends to play music for extra income. When they returned from Cuba, they began to rebuild their houses with complex structured roofs similar to what they saw in Cuba. There were peasants who also lived outside of Les Cayes and did not go to Cuba to stay and work. When those peasants laid eyes on the new roofs their neighbors were building, they were jealous and envious of these musicologist and choreologists. They did not want to admit that the people with nice roofs were superior and more advanced. Instead they ended up going to Cuba also, to work and make some money to enhance their life style. The population outside of Les Cayes even adapted to the Cuban dress code. Now if you go there, you may still see people on the street walking barefoot, and with shitty dress code.

In 1946, when my father first stepped foot on Les Cayes, he observed the people in the entire area and concluded that the population that lived outside of Les Cayes were more sophisticated and more modern than the people who lived outside of Port-au-Prince. Before long this new way of living spread out and developed through the entire country. President Vincent even ordered everyone to wear shoes; no one was allowed to walk barefoot anymore, as they so often did.

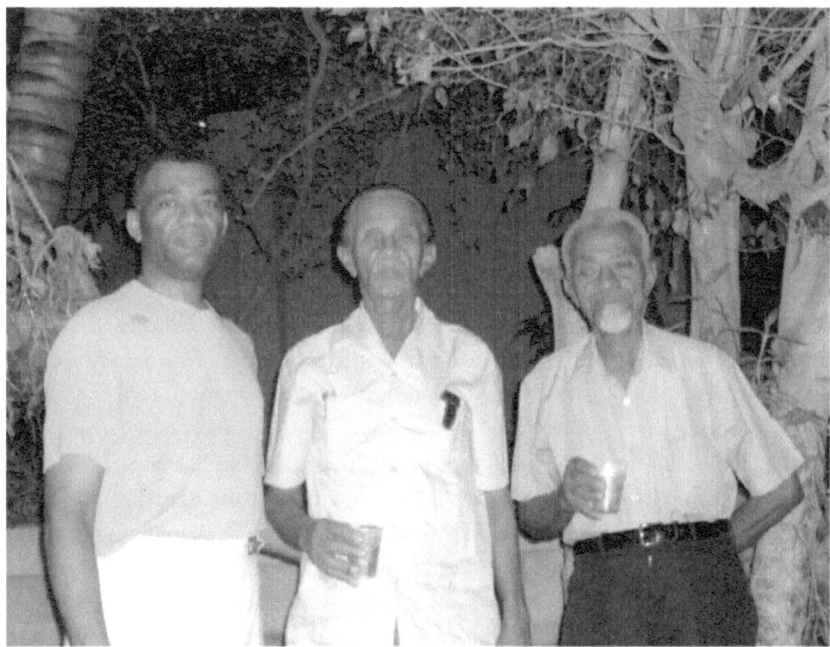

My father was an educator at the age of twenty. President Lescot was side by side with the United States working toward the reorganization of Haiti. Through their efforts, many priests came to live in Haiti and work as educators. The United States sent some soldiers over to Haiti to make sure no harm would come to the priests. To identify where they lived they planted car tires in the road, in front of their homes to protect them in case of war.

When the United States went to Haiti, they created the American institute of agricultural development and many other educational institutes still on the ground. My father was chosen as the chief officer; he was recommended by an English pastor who had a son that went to school with him. But, my father was not trained for the military, so he resigned a few days later. Soon after he left, they called him back to work for them again. He was hired this time as a supervisor of the Haitian farmworkers who worked on a plantation on the countryside. There were seventeen sections of land. Eleven hundred workers were hired to plant crops on each section. He was chosen because he knew the island and the language of the people. He divided the people by groups and trained the most educated one to supervise his own group. In his administration at that time, the southern department state of Haiti was very prosperous.

This is one of the funny stories my father often tells: The workers in the morning before going to work were wasting time standing in front of my father's door. The American office workers at the time were afraid of the people. They closed all the doors of the office buildings, leaving just the windows open. He himself opened his door to get fresh air. He asked, "What's going on? You were supposed to be at the farms." They all replied: you look Haitian and speak many languages with the white men, and you are the only one telling us what to do. He found out they wanted to know how much they had to pay him for hiring them to work at the farm.

My father was so surprised. He never heard of employees having to pay to work. Nothing, he said to them. I gave you work because I need it to be done. Just go to work; that will make me happy. He was young, had no wife, no rent to pay, and made more money than the farmworkers. He ordered them to go; their supervisors were waiting for them. From time to time, the head authorities came to meet with my father and staff. Finally one day they told him, that they did not have to take time to come to Les Cayes for inspections anymore. They had never had any complaints about him from the workers. Everything was always great for business. They promoted him to chief contractor of all the products in and out; his salary jumped higher. But he did not stay too long.

One of his fellow schoolmates was unemployed. During his vacation in the city, they got together. They were recruiting new teachers for the board of education in the urban and established schools in the rural areas as well. Being on vacation, they went together to church to pray before the exams. He accompanied his friend who wanted to take the teaching exams. His friend went inside with all the registration papers required, and my father had to wait outside the professional school where the exams were given. One of my father's old professors from the Lycee passed by and was very surprised to see him. After finding out that my father was working for the American institute for agricultural developments of Haiti, he asked my father to take advantage of a second opportunity by taking the exam as well.

My father thought it was too late. He could not take the exams. He was not sure he could go in without preparation and registration. For him it was impossible. Do not worry, said the professor, knowing you from the Lycee des Cayes, you will do all right. Both went inside meeting with all of my grandfather's friends and colleagues. They all invited my dad to take the exams. One examiner per student, that's how tough it was at that time to earn your qualifications to teach in the school system. He came out first and his friend came out second. Louisdor Jacques, my grandfather, did not understand why my father left the agricultural job to join the school board that paid so much less.

When your score is high in an exam, they give you first choice on where you want to work. His friend being from the outside of the city of Les Cayes wanted to work in the city. My father decided to go to the countryside because he felt the farmworkers needed him. He was very comfortable working toward the education of their children. After a few months of teaching and closer contact with the people, he found out that the Haitian workers at the farm were not dummies. They were only missing direction. That's the reason he spent twenty-five years with the school board working till retirement . . . the best years of my life he said. In his first speech, after being elected mayor of Les Cayes, he said, "I am a citizen from the city and from the countryside as well." After twenty-five years in the rural, he felt closer to rural people than to his own urban colleagues and friends.

In 1946, one of my father's philosophy professors in Les Cayes was campaigning for the presidency. One night my dad woke up; he had a dream about Dumarsais Estime becoming president. He told my grandfather and grandmother about it, and they said to him that Les Cayes will not produce a president. They could not convince my dad who knew Mr. Dumarsais very well. Dumarsais was the prime minister of public instruction (education) when my father was a student at the Lycee. He went to the Lycee to meet with all the professors and do his personal inspection on their work. His professor at that time was incompetent.

My father among other students from Brother Odill Joseph a private school were more advanced in certain subjects such as French literature, English and Spanish languages than his professor of the Lycee. His Professor was jealous. The best students were never given the grades they worked for and deserved. My dad was very upset. One day, he took his corrected exam to his teacher at Brother Odill Joseph, who in turn showed, the paperwork to the Prime Minister Estime. He compared it with three similar papers. The professor gave three different grades. Estime immediately realized that those students' papers had never been corrected properly. Their papers were put in a drawer under students failing list. He went to Les Cayes a week later to meet with all the students; when he asked "how are you doing," they all said "not too bad." Estime's answer was, "I understand your concerns, I will come back to see you all later."

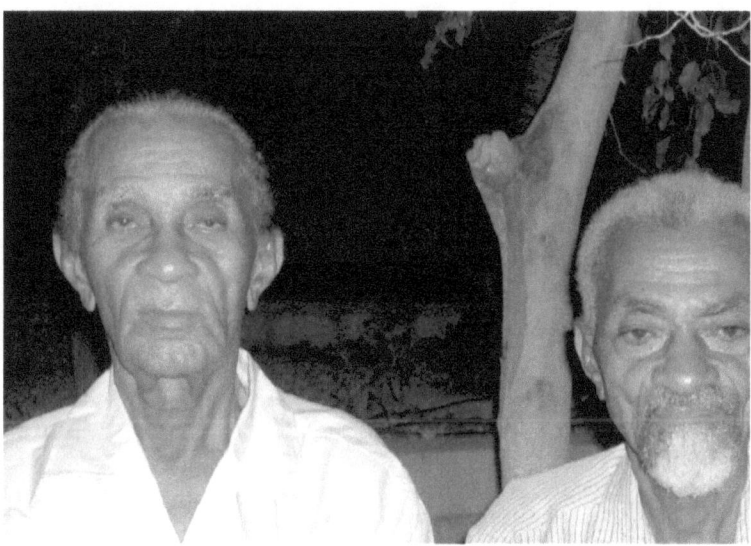

He went to the main office to look at the file cabinet. He realized those drawers had never been opened; they were full of spider' nests. He went straight back to my father's classroom and said "au revoir" to all the students. Two days later he fired all the incompetent professors of the Lycee, replacing them with well-educated ones. As my father said, Nineteen forty-six was the year Haitian ministers truly started doing their job. At that time there were ministers of public instruction in Haiti.

Maurice Dartigue was a minister who specialized in rural education, and Andre Liauteau was a minister who specialized in urban education. Both ministers had scholarships to pursue a study in education overseas, they returned to Haiti to work toward the reorganization of the school system. Lescot was the president at that time. They suggested to the president instead of having two different ministers of instruction, it may be better to have one minister of national educations. They believed that rural and urban education should be combined becoming National Education. However it was never done.

National education has to do in part with culture; there is no culture. Culture is a learning behavior that traditionally you learn as a child from your parents, this is close to nonexistent in Haiti today. Before, the youth had respect for their seniors and parents. Today it's the opposite. The rural people knew they were from outside the city; they took pride in being peasants. They were proud to work in the farms taking care of horses, raising chickens, goats and donkeys, and creating different agricultural products, enough for the wealth of the whole country of Haiti. People in Les Cayes as far as we know had never gone hungry. Now, no matter how much money you have you cannot find anything made in Haiti to buy. From cars to food, all are being imported. Before when you went to your neighbor's house, you had to knock first and wait till you were invited to come in. Now it is different, there is no etiquette. There is a drastic change in behavior, how can we talk about culture? With this change of behavior, culture is nonexistent today.

My father had received a scholarship to study in Belgium, which was not accepted. He decided to pursue his studies in a program at the Institute of Inter-American Affairs designed for educators. In the meantime, Francois Duvalier was campaigning for the presidency. He knew him personally. In 1946, Dr. Duvalier was working for the Institute. My father was recommended by an American friend to work for the same Institute. He was hired as assistant to the chief engineer in the construction department. Dr. Duvalier was placed in the health department office. Whenever someone in the department got sick, my dad called Dr. Duvalier for help. Most of the time, he had to send the patient to him, as my father said, "I spoke to Dr. Duvalier every day over the phone but, we never met each other".

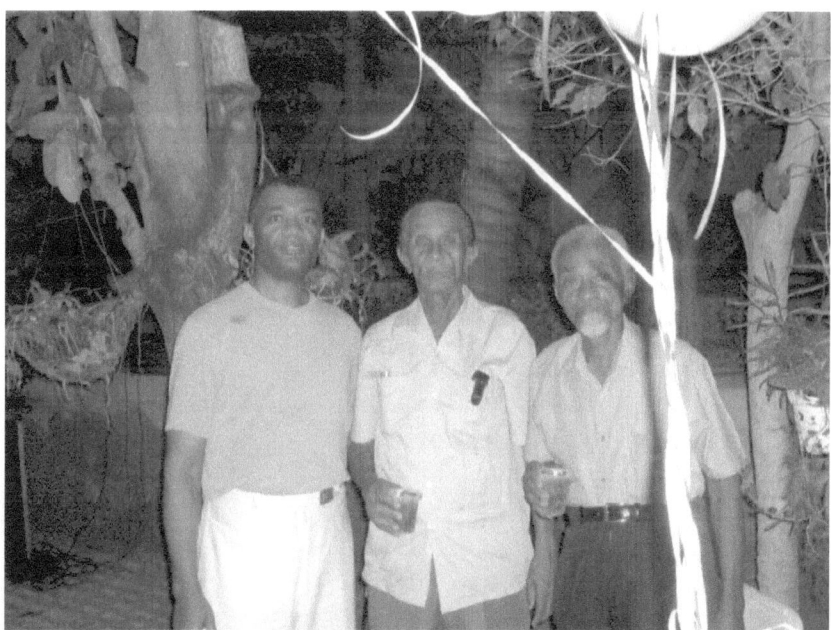

It was not until 1956 that my uncle Anthony Jacques, on vacation in Les Cayes, asked my father, "Among all the candidates, who in your opinion will be elected president." My father's reply was "I will present you to the future president." One of Duvalier's friends volunteered to drive them to meet Duvalier in Port-au-Prince. It was a night in September 1956. They did not get there until 11:00 pm, over eleven hours driving from Les Cayes. They were well received by Dr. Duvalier who wanted to know the reason for the visit. They told him, they knew about the campaign and wanted to see if, they could be helpful to him. Dr. Duvalier said, "If you are from Les Cayes, who told you about me?" He was surprised to know some people from Les Cayes were interested in helping him. After my father told him that he was working for the Institute of Inter-American Affairs in 1946, with him during Estime's time, Duvalier realized who he was and immediately made a gesture. There was no need for bodyguards in the room. The conversation between them never ended that night.

President Magloire who was in power at that time did not want Duvalier to succeed him. He offered $25.000 to whoever gave him Dr. Duvalier's head to eliminate him from the polls. He wanted to be re-elected. He was on good terms with Louis Dejois who was a candidate with 98% of Les Cayes votes. However, when Dejois realized that Magloire wanted to be reelected, he betrayed Magloire. Francois Duvalier was a great politician. Dejois was a great entrepreneur with little knowledge of politics. Both candidates turned out to be good friends.

Finally Dr. Duvalier knew he was going to be president. He said during a meeting held in his home before the election, "Whatever the circumstances, I am the president. I will be elected because God and destiny has chosen me. I am taking the power to install the true social democracy in Haiti." He was very humble, quiet, and never talked too much until 1956 when he became a candidate. He really showed the true color of his hat. Dr. Francois Duvalier was accustomed to listening to a conversation or a speech with his eyes closed, as if he was sleeping and would open his eyes only if he heard something important. He was a great politician, a great ethnologist, and a great doctor. He closed his eyes to avoid wrong answers. If the questions were well put, his answers were always positive.

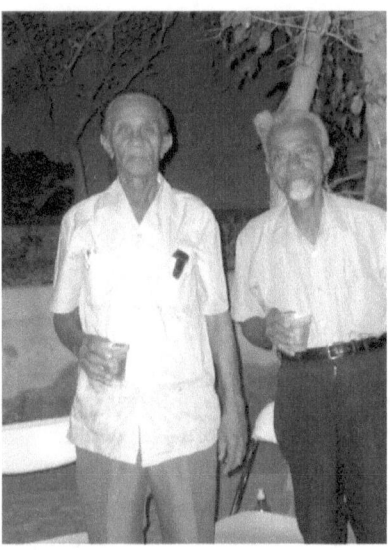

In my father's opinion, it is very rare today to find someone as strong and powerful politically to govern a country as Haiti turned out to be. My father was the first to campaign for Duvalier in Les Cayes. Something he didn't do for a position in politics, but as he said to the president, "It is a service I did for a great Haitian politician and believer in what is right." He read many articles about Dr. Duvalier in many magazines and the journal "les griot". However, my father was an educator, and he remained such as a teacher. Ten years later, Duvalier asked him to join politics as mayor, in Les Cayes by persuading him to take a vacant seat in the city hall. He worked alongside Anthony Milord and Edgar Constant also mayors of Les Cayes. The president did not feel his friend was making enough money teaching. He tried to borrow money to raise educators' salary but was never able to convince the Haitian senate to approve it, so Dr. Duvalier looked after his friend.

The president sent his private helicopter to take my father to Les Cayes for the electoral ceremony. Three months later, he moved him to the post of chief officer of information. Shortly after, my father took the opportunity to develop and build public schools in many rural cities. I was still a little boy. My brothers—Gabriel, Robert, Denis and my sister Yolande went and stayed as well. It was the time, I remember entering elementary school. We all joined hands with everyone in the community and helped in the construction of the schools. We were well received by the community as if we were native in the town of Maniche a suburb of Les Cayes. The memories, the Jacques' family will never forget.

Haiti Earthquake!

In December of 2009, I had an opportunity to spend Christmas in Haiti with my parents, my friend Ginou and I celebrated New-Year's Eve at the Hotel Montana in Port-au-Prince. I had intended to stay in Haiti for a month but, I decided to return earlier. God and destiny were with me because, on January 12, 2010 just two weeks after I returned to Florida a massive earthquake hit Haiti. Had I stayed I would have been at the Club Bellevue on that date with my dear colleague Dominique Richez (the first President of CID Section Haiti) who perished along with many others.

The New Millennium Ballroom

December 31, 1999, I was in Hallandale celebrating the grand opening of the Millennium Ballroom Inc. a name given to the company because 2000 was the millennium. A fifteen-year plan was set to make Hallandale Beach the city my dreams. Unfortunately, two years before I was able to reach my dream, because of the economic situation in the U.S. and around the world my financial situation was tight. At the same time, the landlord raised the lease, it was impossible to pay on time. They stopped me from continuing my operation by changing the locks on all doors, without proper eviction notice.

I lost all my personal properties, gifts, books, instructional videos and curriculum materials, including furniture, original film screen-playwright books and all my investments. God gave me the opportunity to create the Millennium Ballroom, for me and his people to come rejoice and help others improve conditions in their life. I haven't given up, on teaching dance. I decided to start over by setting up a film/video and dance studio program that will attract the general public to Ballroom Dancing.

As a little boy, I finished kindergarten, preparatory school and then, decided to enter secondary school. While living in the USA, I fought to finish college to be better qualified for work. I then fought to earn a master in ballroom dance education in order to become a dance practitioner. Life as I always realized is the largest university of the world with no graduation time. "It's never too late to learn goods". Our head seems to be as large as the whole universe that can hold as much as you are able to put in it. As it is for land, what you put in the earth is exactly what you get. A seed of potato cannot make apricots or tobacco. But I also remember the English saying "No one business is worth the value of what you create."

Doctor-William Rivera, a great supporter and pioneer for many ballroom dance organizations, in 1987, didn't believe ballroom dancing should be part of education and made available to the general public. The year 2005 marked the time I believe, all forms of dance were approved as part of education in every country in the world. What we learn wrong we believe it is right and so, we will always do it wrong. Scientists all over the world are people who learn and believe in what is right and always do it right, never wrong. The inclusion of dance in the schooling system was made possible in part by CID (International dance council) one of the umbrella organizations for all forms of dance in the world. It is also the organization that inspired me to write this book my perceptual filters about me, my mother and father, my Haitian brothers and sisters and the country of my birth

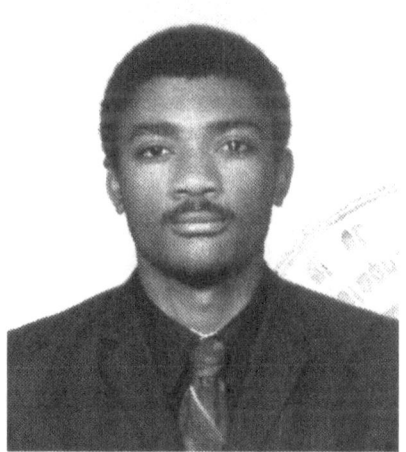

Michel F. Jacques
Autobiography /

I was born in Haiti. My sign is Libra, my mother Macilia St-Paul and Father Legagneur E. Jacques. **I started my career by learning basic dance movements at an early age in Les Cayes-Haiti. To me, it was a very natural part of my life style and I considered it an entertaining and challenging hobby. In 1980, I began my exploration of ballroom dancing at the Policar International Dance Institute in Port-au-Prince, Haiti. I also developed my skills and talents in journalism at** Tele-Haiti where I gained invaluable expertise in the field of video production. To me, the role of dance is unique in maintaining a national and cultural identity.

In 1984, I ventured to the United States to pursue and further develop a career in film directing. I decided to join the Arthur Murray Board of educators in its rigorous teaching training program. With the demands and challenges of the program, and as a social dance instructor, I achieved a greater understanding of the significance and impact dance would have on my life. I arduously studied and graduated with a Music and Video Business degree (MVB) from the prestigious Art Institute of Fort Lauderdale, Florida. I developed a teaching system that conveyed to my students an understanding that musical rhythms are cultural representations.

www.ingramcontent.com/pod-product-compliance
Lightning Source LLC
Chambersburg PA
CBHW032018170526
45157CB00002B/756